PURSUED
by the
SHEPHERD

PURSUED

by the

SHEPHERD

Every Woman's Journey
from Lost to Found

KARON PHILLIPS
GOODMAN

Revell
Grand Rapids, Michigan

For my husband. You can't lose me.

Contents

INTRODUCTION

Suppose one of you has a hundred sheep and loses one of them. Does he not leave the ninety-nine in the open country and go after the lost sheep until he finds it? And when he finds it, he joyfully puts it on his shoulders and goes home. Then he calls his friends and neighbors together and says, "Rejoice with me; I have found my lost sheep."

Luke 15:4–6

How many times have I been the hundredth sheep? How many times have I wandered away, alone and confused? How many times have I ignored the Lord's map and followed my own directions to the wrong place? That same number of times, He's come looking for me. I think God must have the world's largest lost-and-found department. I've visited there quite often, but it's never a permanent stay. I can never get so lost the Lord won't find me.

We don't usually get lost in the parking lot (well, I do), but we regularly get lost in our own sadness or guilt or confusion or misjudgment. We detour away from God's grace and power and try to navigate ourselves. It's a senseless turn, so He comes to rescue us. He comes after me every time.

He follows me and speaks my name and waits for me to turn around in answer to His call. It's as if He sees my broken heart far more clearly than all I've broken in my path. It's my heart He pursues, my link to Him that I feel I have no right to claim. But His calls

11

get louder and more urgent, and my heart dares to believe again. I turn around and look at Him, and, amazingly, He lifts me over the debris of my lostness and hugs me to Him. I am found, and the reunion begins. We can explore together, and He directs the growing and becoming of His faithful though faulty disciple.

Jesus' story says the shepherd called his friends and neighbors to share in his happiness. Wow. I'd think the Lord would want to hide me when He found me weathered and worn, at least until He could scrub me up pretty good and give me a bit of a makeover. But no, God doesn't hide us no matter how pitiful we look after our lostness. Instead He calls us to use that very moment, to be an example and a promise of all that's to come. The reunion isn't a finish line but a launching pad.

Have you ever been the hundredth sheep? Probably so, because it's easy to get lost, isn't it? And it's our own personal miracle when we're found. We're held close to our Shepherd, redeemed and changed, ready to walk with Him renewed and awakened, ready to follow our Guide who is *never* lost. Travel with me here for a while, won't you? The scenery just keeps getting better and better.

Part 1

MISGUIDED

> Therefore the people wander like sheep oppressed for lack of a shepherd.
>
> Zechariah 10:2

Sometimes we behave as if we have no map for this journey of our lives, as if our Shepherd forgot to discuss a few crucial turns with us. The path is winding and the decision ours, and on shaky feet and fuzzy thoughts we step away from His guidance—and then wonder what happened. We have to look back before we can travel ahead.

We don't suddenly wake up "lost"—it usually takes us a while to get there. We sometimes don't even realize how badly off course we are, but it happens all the time, with or without our awareness. Don't you wish there was a flashing neon sign that would pop up in front of us and shout, "Stop! Wrong way, little sheep!" That would be helpful, wouldn't it? Or something like a nutrition label that wouldn't let us forget there were a zillion calories in that brownie—now that would do it. But instead we mosey along, oblivious to or defiant of any warning signs, and we awaken in the darkness. How'd we get there?

Sheep cannot be left alone. No wonder our watchful Shepherd compares us to them so often. The hapless creatures can't be trusted! They need fences and troughs and barns and, most of all, a Shepherd to rescue them when they lose their way. They need a Shepherd to unleash the great potential hidden within their vast weaknesses. They need to be found.

Our Shepherd does that for us all the time, somehow knowing how to deal with our tendency to wander into other pastures despite the bounty of our own.

While a little sheep may not be an expert at much, she knows all about getting lost. I can relate. It's so easy to become influenced by our world, to allow ourselves to be pulled this way and that, to make questionable moves and then complain about the not-so-great land we stumble into. So many directions are open to us every moment, some leading to small detours and some leading farther off the path than we can imagine. And even armed with the knowledge of home and all that it provides, we often follow every one of those wrong paths.

Like the little pea-brained sheep, we trot after the day's special and see if this time we're smarter than that built-in radar that connects us to the Shepherd and guides us flawlessly when we allow it to. We shake our fuzzy little heads and try to outwit or ignore the God-given sense of direction we need because we're—well, because we're sheep, unencumbered by any excess wisdom that would make our pasture nibbling easier. Far be it for us to choose a more peaceful procession through the clover.

But because Jesus is forever patient and not bothered by explaining to us things a grasshopper could grasp, He finds us for the hundredth time to remind us that we are sheep *with* a Shepherd. And He understands our lostness and rejoices in our foundness, while we once again realize that sheep who appear to know so little need to know only one thing—how to follow their Shepherd.

May we learn it a little better this time.

For Reflection

What goes on in your mind when you ponder the different directions you can take?

When have you wandered as if you were a sheep without a Shepherd?

My Shepherd who guides me, please forgive my misguided attempts to navigate for myself. Stay so close in front of me that I can see only You. Amen.

1

MISGUIDED . . . BY MISTIMING

As Paul discoursed on righteousness, self-control and the judgment
to come, Felix was afraid and said, "That's enough for now! You may
leave. When I find it convenient, I will send for you."

Acts 24:25

Sometimes our lostness simply begins by being late because we neglect the signs, those silent ones tugging at our hearts. That's what
Felix did. As governor of Caesarea, Felix listened to the case against
Paul, that he was a "troublemaker" (Acts 24:5) who professed belief
in Christ and His resurrection. And Felix listened to Paul witness
about his faith in the living God more than once. Paul's passionate
and unwavering testimony was a little too much for the governor,
and he was afraid to search his own heart for Christ. So he put it
off, wanting to wait for a more "convenient" time.

Oh, how many times have we done that? Maybe not with our
very salvation, but with other pullings of the Spirit we've delayed
answering. Unlike Paul, we neglect or ignore the directions God
gives us. We decide that "some other time later on, when I feel

better" will be more convenient, and so we become like Felix and send the thoughts away.

We're also misguided by our fears of the unknown. Jesus is waiting to lead us, but our mistiming keeps Him apart, like a shadow. We run off to where it's more comfortable, where the path of least resistance is the path to lostness.

Sometimes that's in the "but I'm not good enough for that" pasture or the "when I get such and such done" pasture. Hiding is more convenient to our "I need to tend to this now" lives than accepting what our Lord stands to offer us. And that's a tragedy. We miss out on deep blessings and the closeness of Christ available to us in a single breath when we're misguided by mistiming. We put off the One who wants only to lift us up. And it's dark in the lost land of mistimed choices.

For Reflection

What do you keep saying "That's enough for now!" about?

What are you afraid of? Is it bigger than God?

If God touched you with only one blessing a day, how many blessings will you have missed because you've been waiting for a more "convenient" time to follow Him?

> *My Shepherd who guides me, please help me
> remember that what is convenient for You is blessing
> to me. Please heal me from my mistimed wanderings.
> Amen.*

2

Misguided . . . by Misvalue

"Go, sell everything you have and give to the poor, and you will have treasure in heaven. Then come, follow me." At this the man's face fell. He went away sad, because he had great wealth.

Mark 10:21–22

We all hear this story and think, "Well, that's not me, because I'm certainly not rich!" Neither was the ruler of the story—not really, not in the ways that count—but he was desperate to hold on to all he had. Jesus asked him to give up everything on the spot. It probably wouldn't have mattered if Jesus had asked for only half or a quarter of all the young man held. The man simply valued his "great wealth" above all else, rejecting a Shepherd who would value *him* above all else. That's a good way to get lost.

Sometimes we reject God's prodding just because we're not willing to give up something we value. He can tell us what He's offering is worth far more than what we hold so tightly, but it doesn't seem to matter. We can't see beyond what's blocking our steps. Like fake boulders used in movies—those that look heavy as earth and weigh three pounds—what we see as valuable is really powerless. Until we make it so.

Then we're misguided by our misvaluing of what we hold dear, and its power is scary because we reject the value of God's offering. Like the rich young ruler, we lose our way, valuing something that doesn't value us.

Often our misguidance seems harmless. We value the security we place in tangible things and resources—and that's not so bad because God calls us to be responsible. But we're misguided when we let that value supplant instead of supplement our security in God.

We value our free will to live as we choose—and that's not so bad because God gave us free will. But we're misguided when we forget that our God-given gift of choice works best within, not in defiance of, His control.

We value our abilities—and that's not so bad because God didn't make our lights to shine under baskets. But we're misguided when we believe those abilities exist outside His grace.

When we're misguided by our misvalue of all we hold so tightly, we're lost to the stranglehold, not the support, of those things. With the same fear the young ruler had, we take detours into the dark land of all we've deemed too valuable and precious to trade in for something else. But that something else—letting God call us "His"—is far more valuable than all we claim as "ours."

For Reflection

What do you hold so tightly?

How much power does this "wealth" have on you?

What Jesus offered the ruler was of so much more value than his money, but he wouldn't see it. When have you failed to see what He was offering you?

> *My Shepherd who guides me, please show me the*
> *real value of myself in Your eyes. Help me see that*
> *reflection and release my heart from misvalued things*
> *that lead me astray. Amen.*

3

MISGUIDED . . . BY MISUSE

Then the man who had received the one talent came. "Master," he said . . . "I was afraid and went out and hid your talent in the ground. See, here is what belongs to you." His master replied, "You wicked, lazy servant! . . . Take the talent from him and give it to the one who has the ten talents. For everyone who has will be given more, and he will have an abundance. Whoever does not have, even what he has will be taken from him. And throw that worthless servant outside, into the darkness."

Matthew 25:24–26, 28–30

Nothing about living a God-filled life is about fear. It's all about the joyous willingness to risk everything we see because of our faith in everything we don't. It's being guided to use all we are to advance all He wants, knowing that what we use will come back to us as more. Still, we get lost sometimes, like the chastised servant, misguided by our misuse of the tools He's given us. It's a lostness always grounded in fear.

Maybe we're afraid even to find out what God has planned for our lives. Maybe we're afraid we won't be able to find out or, worse, that we won't know what to do next when we do find out. Maybe we're afraid we'll make more mistakes and fail in our part of His plan. Maybe we're afraid we won't be perfect, so we don't try at all.

Yet by living in that fear, we do fail—not because our efforts aren't enough, but because we don't make any. Our misuse lands us in a dark pit where our gifts wither on the vine, out of the sun.

What the other two servants in the story did pleased the master because they used what they had and followed what he had taught them. They were unafraid and willing to step out in their faith. That's all our Master asks of us—not to be better than someone else or an example of perfection, but to use what we have and follow Him in whatever mighty way He's chosen. And our walk with God waits to become mighty when we use it as He's planned.

If we don't walk where He's leading but instead follow our fear, we get lost, and we lose the untamed joy of being a part of our Father's plan. We lose that connection with Him because we fail to claim it.

Using what we have won't always—or even often—mean something grand or impressive as the world sees it. But it does mean doing everything we do without fear and with the abilities God's given us. Getting lost is what happens when we don't.

For Reflection

What gifts have you buried out of fear?

Where were you misguided by misuse of your gifts in the past?

Why do you think God gave you special and unique gifts, and what makes you afraid to use them?

> *My Shepherd who guides me, please know I want to*
> *use everything You've given me and not waste a bit.*
> *Make me eager and unafraid to produce a bounty*
> *through Your blessing and not misuse one gift. Amen.*

4

Misguided . . . by Misjudgment

Then Saul said to Samuel, "I have sinned. I violated the LORD's command and your instructions."

1 Samuel 15:24

While Felix was afraid to hear too much of God's message, King Saul of Israel judged his own interpretation of the message better than the Lord's. Arrogance became his attitude, and he misjudged God's reaction to his choices. He obeyed God—sort of—and judged that enough. It cost him his kingdom, and we read why in 1 Samuel 15.

God commanded Saul to attack the Amalekites, evil people who had tortured the Israelites on their way to the Promised Land. And that part Saul did. But he didn't follow through.

"Now go, attack the Amalekites and totally destroy everything that belongs to them. Do not spare them; put to death men and women, children and infants, cattle and sheep, camels and donkeys" (1 Sam. 15:3). The battle was fierce, but the command fell incomplete. Saul captured rather than killed the king of the terrorists, Agag, and saved the best of the livestock to sacrifice to God.

Saul judged his sacrifice better than his obedience, but he was wrong. "Does the LORD delight in burnt offerings and sacrifices as much as in obeying the voice of the LORD? To obey is better than sacrifice, and to heed is better than the fat of rams" (v. 22).

Have we been guilty of this kind of misguidance? Yes, and it's not always with the worst of intentions. "This just seems better," we say, or, "It makes more sense this way." That's what leads us to justify whatever pops into our heads, maybe not out of malice but out of poor judgment. Then the arrogance takes over, and before we know it, we're sitting on a monument to our own wisdom—and it's a lonely place.

When we substitute our judgment for God's, we're wandering astray, steeped in our own inflated importance. And we have no idea what it will cost us when we're lost.

Our orders today won't be to annihilate a whole gang of people and farm animals, but they come just as clear and with just as much expectation: "Follow Me." Never does "unless you think your way is better" come after.

For Reflection

In what ways do you think maybe you know better than God?

What do you say to yourself to justify your choices?

What "kingdom" have you lost because of your misjudgment?

> *My Shepherd who guides me, please help me*
> *understand that Your commands are perfect and I*
> *need not add anything to them except my obedience.*
> *Help me past my misjudgment and on to Your will.*
> *Amen.*

5

MISGUIDED . . . BY MISTAKES

"Have you eaten from the tree that I commanded you not to eat from?" The man said, "The woman you put here with me—she gave me some fruit from the tree, and I ate it." Then the LORD God said to the woman, "What is this you have done?" The woman said, "The serpent deceived me, and I ate."

Genesis 3:11–13

Well, isn't that just like us?

"It was all her fault, Lord!"

"Uh-uh, God, don't blame me!"

Adam and Eve made mistakes, but they sure didn't want to admit it. Who knows what would have happened if they'd said, "Yes, Father, we're both to blame but ask for Your mercy and grace"?

Instead they were misguided by their mistakes. Wishing they could change the past but unable to, they tried to shift the blame. Don't we do that sometimes? We look for a reason or excuse for what happened—it was somebody else's fault—so we don't have to shoulder our part of the blame. And instead of resting in God's grace, we're lost in our attempts to confuse Him. Like Adam and Eve, we hide, so burdened by our mistakes that we take another wrong turn and run away from Him instead of toward Him.

When have you let your shame about something steer you away from your Shepherd? Have you blamed others for your actions, hoping their grievances were somehow bad enough to take the spotlight off you? Offering up someone else's sins won't mitigate your own.

When we play the "she's worse than I am" game, we're running away from one of God's most beautiful expressions of His love—the grace that takes those mistakes and turns them into something else. He's a master at transforming regret into renewal, ego into empathy, selfishness into surrender. That's the lighted path to follow, but when we're misguided by our mistakes and let them instead of God rule us, they become ours to keep forever. And they're cold company in the dark lostness.

For Reflection

What mistakes have guided you away from God instead of toward Him?

How does it feel to carry those mistakes with you every step you take?

How have you tried to sacrifice others to save yourself, and how has doing so failed to deliver the relief you wanted?

> *My Shepherd who guides me, please help me reveal myself to You—all the good, the bad, and the ugly. Help me understand that You already see all and stand ready to forgive my mistakes if I'll follow You instead of them. Amen.*

6

MISGUIDED . . . BY MISDIRECTION

> I do not understand what I do. For what I want to do I do not do,
> but what I hate I do. . . . For I have the desire to do what is good, but
> I cannot carry it out. For what I do is not the good I want to do; no,
> the evil I do not want to do—this I keep on doing.
>
> Romans 7:15, 18–19

We can really identify with Paul on this one, can't we? We want to do better and show kindness and grow wiser, but we don't. We don't want to hurt others or live selfishly or choose poorly, but we do. We don't want to get lost or wander away from our Shepherd or wake up feeling cold and alone, but we do.

Paul understood the war we all fight within, to embrace the good and resist the bad. He knew we'd face that struggle because of the world we live in and our own weaknesses, all of which try to misguide us every moment. And when we give in to the pressure and follow the misdirection away from God's hand, we have the result of a lost struggle, a lost *us*.

The misdirection we take, allowing just a bit of deviation from God's pasture, may lead us to be judgmental and cruel. Or it may go further into a life of hate and anger. Maybe we'll fail to see the wonder around us and become comfortable in our complaints, bitterness, and self-pity. We could even get so far away from the pasture that we speak out in abusive ways to others and kill their dreams. The most unintended misdirection can at any time lead us to a troubled lostness. When we find ourselves there, we know we've lost the battle again, and we can't find the guiding light.

Then we wonder if God is surprised, if He's noticed we've wandered off in the opposite direction, away from the peace He promised. We don't know, because we often spend a lot of time justifying our choices, calling that lack of peace "part of life" or "one of those things" or something that makes it seem like we didn't have a choice.

Misnaming our misdirection isn't the way out of it, but looking for a Savior is. "Who will rescue me?" Paul asks (Rom. 7:24), and so do we. Who can guide us through this land of many choices so that we do what pleases God?

All of the misdirection in the world, from little sidetracks to cross-country jogs, isn't enough to lose us from our Shepherd. We can go the wrong way for one step or a thousand, but it doesn't change the way back. Misguided by our misdirection, we're lost and in pain, but that doesn't have to last.

For Reflection

Have you been misguided by your misdirection in a small way or a big way?

Did you plan your wrong turn in advance or feel you made a spontaneous decision?

What have you called your misdirection in the past?

*My Shepherd who guides me, please help me do
what I should and not do what I shouldn't. Help
me see that any misdirection produces an emptiness
that hurts and can be filled only by Your peace.
Amen.*

7

MISGUIDED ... BY MISTRUST

The devil said to him, "If you are the Son of God, tell this stone to become bread." Jesus answered, "It is written: 'Man does not live on bread alone.'" The devil led him up to a high place and showed him in an instant all the kingdoms of the world. . . . "If you worship me, it will all be yours." Jesus answered, "It is written: 'Worship the Lord your God and serve him only.'"

Luke 4:3–5, 7–8

The devil, in whatever form he takes, wants us to follow our trust in ourselves instead of God, to separate us from our Shepherd. When the devil tempted Jesus for forty days, he did it with an appeal to Jesus' human side, but Jesus surprised him and responded to his every temptation with the Word of God. "Full of the Holy Spirit" (Luke 4:1), He was guided by His trust in His Father. Can we always say the same?

Sometimes we're misguided by our very human mistrust when we're faced with temptations, challenges, or troubles, and we trust ourselves instead of our Father. Then the land we find ourselves in is empty and parched, yet it sucks us down like quicksand.

It seems easier somehow to put our trust in what we can see and touch—our own possessions or accomplishments or assets. It even seems reasonable to think God would want us to trust in what He's given us. But Jesus chose not to use His own power against the devil's temptations, and so can we. We can choose to trust in God's power.

Of course, that sounds very surreal, like a platitude meant to soothe nerves and offer no real hope. But trust in God's power is what enables us to face all that threatens any part of our lives with a confidence and calm that sheep feel because they have a shepherd. It's looking in unquestioning faith beyond any temptation or trial to our lives held in His hands before, after, and always.

Trust in ourselves produces only a veiled confidence, one at risk of collapsing if the stakes get too high or the devil gets too good at his work. Don't we know that everything we are and have exists at the pleasure and will of God? As solid or powerful as what we control might look, it is as transparent as air, as intangible as a thought.

And when we're misguided by our mistrust, we live with that nagging fear that we're not as smart and together as we thought we were. Trust in God, though, reveals the way at just the right moment, with just the right response, as with Jesus in the desert. It's a power to send the tempter away and bring us closer to God. But we sometimes let our trust in ourselves win, and then we are lost.

For Reflection

When you trust in your power instead of God's, how secure do you feel?

When have you done that lately?

Why do you think you make that choice at times and give such power to your misguided trust?

How far away from God does that choice make you feel?

My Shepherd who guides me, please deliver me from weak trust in myself and fill me with the Holy Spirit so that I will not mistrust again. Help me answer all temptations and stumbles with Your infallible Word. Amen.

Part 2

LOST

For the Son of Man came to seek and to save what was lost.

Luke 19:10

Following every kind of misguidance, large or small, is lostness for our hearts, a separation from God. The result may come from one misguided choice or a whole batch mixed together. It doesn't matter. Anytime we're anywhere except putting our foot directly into the footprint God has just made, we're lost.

Sometimes we're a little lost, and one turn is all we need to get back to our pasture. Other times we're a lot lost, and we think it'll take a king's army to find us. Either extreme, or anywhere in between, hurts and threatens to take away our hope and faith. Yet our Shepherd is the same distance away. We just can't see Him because we're misled into the darkness.

The silly little sheep follows anything that catches her eye, wanders off to poke around in this clover patch or that trickling stream, and never looks back as she walks in the wrong direction. Then she gazes up for a moment, wrinkles her brow at the unfamiliar territory, and realizes she sees no fence post, no rolling hill that looks like her path home. She is lost. And she must make some decisions.

The little sheep's first decision is probably to bleat loudly and stomp her hoof in anger at the ground for leading her astray. We do the same. It's as if we wake up mad at the whole universe, maybe even questioning our worthiness to be in it, given our poor sense of direction.

And where is the God of our pasture anyway? We haven't thought about Him much during our wanderings. He was "close enough," we reasoned to ourselves, while He was quiet and watching. But now He seems distant, absent in the dark. Who moved? How did this happen?

Oh yeah, that's right. We can look back at all the misguidance that led us here if we want. We know it well enough—we lived it and have the scars to prove it. We made those choices, and it won't do any good to blame anyone else. I need not bother to point my finger at my husband or my best friend or a co-worker. I need not make a list of problems and pressures that presented themselves. I chose the path that misled me here, and I'll only get more lost, deeper into the darkness, if I focus on anything other than my own misguided steps of misplaced trust, bad timing, or thoughtless choice.

So what's often the little sheep's next decision, when screaming and stomping and complaining don't help? She tries to find her way out of the darkness by herself. How hard could it be? We think the same way. We got ourselves lost, so surely we can get ourselves found, back to the same safe place we left.

But is that place still there? Has the Shepherd carried His flock to a better place? Has He failed to notice or forgotten He's missing someone? Has He moved the universe along without *me*? What if there's no place for me at home—if I ever find home again? What then?

Panic sets in because we intuitively know the truth: home isn't the same. It will be changed because we're changed in the darkness. We can't "lose" our lostness. We can only hope for a rescue.

> You, O LORD, keep my lamp burning; my God turns my darkness into light. With your help I can advance against a troop; with my God I can scale a wall.
>
> Psalm 18:28–29

For Reflection

How do you react when you find yourself lost?

Whom do you blame for the wrong turn?

What do you do first?

> *My Shepherd who sees in the dark, please don't forsake Your wayward sheep. Rescue me from any place You wouldn't choose for me, and guide my way home. Amen.*

8

THE DARKNESS OF LOST HUMILITY

Two men went up to the temple to pray, one a Pharisee and the other a tax collector. The Pharisee stood up and prayed about himself: "God, I thank you that I am not like other men—robbers, evildoers, adulterers—or even like this tax collector. I fast twice a week and give a tenth of all I get." But the tax collector stood at a distance. He would not even look up to heaven, but beat his breast and said, "God, have mercy on me, a sinner." I tell you that this man, rather than the other, went home justified before God. For everyone who exalts himself will be humbled, and he who humbles himself will be exalted.

Luke 18:10–14

Sometimes it's getting lost when we least expect it that hurts and confuses us the most. It's when we think we're "above" certain behaviors or mistakes, when we think we're so much better than others, that we fall into a darkness of shame and grief. It happens when we think we're doing just fine without God too close, because we're quite comfortable in our faith.

But actually we're complacent, too distracted to examine how we're feeling, quite sure we've got it all together, or too busy to find out if we really do. We can get lost like this anytime for a whole bunch of reasons.

There's somebody worse. Especially when we're overwhelmed with our responsibilities and everybody down to the dog is demanding more and more, we're likely to get lost like this. We look at all our stress, throw our hands up in the air in exasperation, and say, "Well, at least I'm doing better than so-and-so!"

What we're saying is "I may not be perfect, but so-and-so isn't either." While that may be true, it misses the point. It doesn't ease our frustration. What so-and-so does isn't important in your walk with God. What *you* do is, because God's always searching for that attitude of humility. What's in your heart when you do your job, tend to your family, pray your prayers? With what kind of slate do you go to God to discuss your life? Do you bring others' tallies with you?

When we compare ourselves to others, like the Pharisee, we're looking to make ourselves superior because it makes us feel better. If we make a hot supper tonight for everybody, are we better than so-and-so's mom who went through the drive-through? That kind of comparison—trying to outdo someone on a scale we invent—is a darkness of lost humility because it traps us in a world where our opinion is more important than God's; our opinion revolves around us and keeps us from revolving around Him. When we decide what makes us worthy, we decide we can judge others as well. That's not our job.

Not me! Sometimes we're quick to judge because we feel we're "safe" with some absolutes, that we can predict with 100 percent certainty some things that will or won't happen to us. But when things don't follow our prediction, what next? We don't know where to go because we've convinced everyone, including ourselves, that we'd never need to know, that we'd never be here in this place others have visited.

Maybe you never thought you'd lose your temper with your children or be tempted by drugs or alcohol. What if you bragged about your material possessions and now you're deep in debt? Or what if you believed your marriage was strong but now it's crumbling beneath you? What if . . . ? The list goes on and on.

Sometimes we get too secure in ourselves, forgetting we're fallible and subject to the world's influences all the time. We don't know if we'll be exactly like others, as the Pharisee disputed, but we can be sure the possibility is there because we're all weak sheep who can elevate ourselves a bit too high at times. Banking on our own righteousness to make us strong will never work.

I'm hitting my marks, so everything's good. The Pharisee was proud of his fasting and tithing, and he used that measurement basically to demand favor from God. Sometimes we can do the same, when we claim we're following so closely the letter of the law that everything in our lives should also.

But what will the Pharisee have to hold him when everything doesn't go smoothly? He prays not to get closer to God but for God to recognize his less-than-heartfelt efforts—outward signs that mean nothing if there is no humility and worship to accompany them.

When we let our church attendance or committee service or anything others see become the benchmark by which we measure our progress on our walk with God, we're lost. Certainly these things are valuable, but they can lure us into a false sense of importance and security: "I'm living right, so I'm okay, and God should reward that."

Well, maybe so, maybe not. Do your fasting and tithing or other outward acts come from your heart or from your hunt for approval and accolade? If no one could see your actions, would you still do the same things that look like devotion to God? And do you point out your service to God regularly so He doesn't forget, in case He wants to give you something?

Of course, unless you live in an igloo in the Arctic, others are going to see your choices, and that's not something to avoid. But are they seeing something that reflects your heart or something that reflects your ego? All of the things we do "for God" and "in the name of God" come from somewhere.

Sometimes it's from a darkness of lost humility that says, "Look at me—see how great I am" instead of "Look at God—see how great He is." And the loss of that partnership with our Shepherd that we could have if we'd only ask is an emptiness no human recognition can fill.

Lost Possibilities

A long time ago I wanted a job so much that I went to the place and pretty much annoyed my way in after the owner told me several times he wasn't looking for any help. But in a few weeks, I had the job I wanted so badly. I decided they'd love me like their own and knew I'd be there forever.

It lasted about six weeks. It was the only time I was ever fired. It still hurts to think about it.

I couldn't believe he'd fire me. I thought, *How could he not want me? How could he think I was too stupid to work for him? How could I lose this job?* I don't know what all I did wrong, except that I do know there was absolutely no humility in me where that job was concerned. There was no willingness in me to say, "Have a little mercy on me, please. I'm like everybody else and I need help." It never occurred to me that I couldn't have it my way.

Now, years away from that horrible experience, I blame myself for losing that job I wanted more than anything. At the time, I missed all the signs and kept plowing deeper and deeper into the darkness until the owner left me there. I was unwilling to be led out and perhaps, as he said, incapable not so much of learning but of being taught. Gulp.

That situation was my loss, and I wonder how many times I've made similar choices with my heavenly Father. How many times has He presented an opportunity and I've said, "No thanks if I can't have it my way," when I could have been blessed in countless ways? Have you ever done that?

In little ways, we probably all have, by being like the Pharisee and assuming we know what's in someone else's heart. He didn't know the tax collector's heart, muddled in business not his own, and ended up lost. If I'm too worried about comparing my heart to someone else's or glorifying my own efforts, I'll be lost too.

I have enough to examine in my own heart; I can't examine another person's too. But I can reverse the Pharisee-thinking concept. Instead of "Thank You, God, I am not like everybody else," I can pray, "Thank You, God, I *am* just like everybody else, and I know You love me despite my mistakes and imperfections." Instead of baaing about all I do, I can ask, "What pleases *You*, Lord? What guides me closer to *Your* plan for my life?"

It might be hard to let go of our Pharisee attitude at first, but we can do it when our focus changes from us to our Shepherd. And it's much brighter there as we bow down at His knee, ready to grow.

Do not gloat over me, my enemy! Though I have fallen, I will rise. Though I sit in darkness, the LORD will be my light.

Micah 7:8

For Reflection

How have you felt when you wandered in the darkness of lost humility?

How is your thinking ever like the Pharisee's?

How close do you feel to God when you're tooting your self-righteous horn?

My Shepherd who sees in the dark, please forgive my focus on what I've done for You instead of what You do for me every moment. Help me understand Your delight in a humble attitude, and please help my heart reflect Your light. Amen.

9

THE DARKNESS OF
LOST PRIORITIES

Yet at the same time many even among the leaders believed in [Jesus].
But because of the Pharisees they would not confess their faith for
fear they would be put out of the synagogue; for they loved praise
from men more than praise from God.

John 12:42–43

Those pesky Pharisees again. A powerful religious group in Jesus'
time, they were sticklers for detail and doing things the way only
they interpreted as right. Many Jews with less power and position followed them despite believing Jesus' message because their
religious lives touched everything else they did. They feared the
Pharisees because they had a lot of clout and could make the lives
of those who stepped outside their thin lines miserable.

So, misguided by a misplaced loyalty, those who heard Jesus
refused Him and instead wandered into a darkness where their
souls were at stake. We do this today—we give in to peer pressure

because we want "praise from men" or maybe because it's easier, but that slope is downhill all the way.

Today, evidence of our lost priorities may not be as visible or tangible as walking away from Jesus, but it's alive in our hearts and minds and shows itself in the kind of lives we lead.

Sometimes the darkness of expectations and obligations closes in on us and we're afraid to look beyond the next step, afraid of what we can't see, so we let others' priorities become our own, others who claim to know more than we do or wield some kind of power. This darkness is following a course away from your Shepherd that you don't want or believe in because "they" say it's the right direction.

Like a robot, we follow preprogrammed commands and don't dare shake a screw loose. But we're not robots, and we don't have to be lost in this darkness. Jesus said, "I have come into the world as a light, so that no one who believes in me should stay in darkness" (John 12:46).

Believing is the key. And it's so much more than acknowledging He lives.

You know that it's your responsibility to choose between the brownie and the banana, between the extra twenty minutes of sleep and getting ready for the day without a lot of stress and panic. Those are easy priorities to identify. You know the price and it's your choice to pay it or not.

But what about the other lost priorities—those of the heart where we let something other than our best intentions guide us? See if you picture yourself in any of these situations, all based on fear.

Fear of others seeing you fail. What would you attempt if no one could see? We don't live in a vacuum, so others will see when the limb we race out on breaks. Have you let your priority of not failing keep you from following your Shepherd? Have you been afraid to believe God's urgings because you were afraid you might be wrong? Is it more important to call no attention to yourself than to risk someone seeing you as imperfect?

Like when we jump up after a fall and see if anyone was watching, if we worry way too much about what someone else sees and way too little about what our Father wants *us* to see, we're lost in that darkness where we see nothing.

Fear of losing comfort. Sometimes following God's lead isn't comfortable. He may send us over rocky terrain where the natives aren't so friendly. And we might see that trial coming and instead stay behind in the pasture we know by heart. The trouble is, God may have a greener pasture in mind for us, but by going nowhere, we can't find it.

We may still be in familiar and safe territory, but it's a bit dark now, and even though we didn't want anything to change, everything is changing. The comfort we loved so much is fading. Have you been lost in that darkness, where what you thought was so wonderful turned out to be a lonely prison? Whether it's comfort from our position or money or job that we fear losing, the greater loss is when God wants to lead us closer to Him but we refuse.

Exchanging the comfort we thought we had for God's lead, though, is a new, most wonderful kind of comfort—one where we feel Him so close, because if we *ever* follow Him with just one step, we discover He's like air: we can't escape Him, and even when we hold our breath in momentary fear, He's still inside us. The darkness opposite that comfort is fear that won't stop.

Fear of losing control. Oh, this is me. Don't get me wrong, I don't want to control *your* life—unless it touches mine. Then I'll decide what's best and let you know. And it would be in your best interest to just go along with whatever I say. There, see how simple things can be?

Sometimes I want to treat God the same way. Maybe you feel like that too. Are you afraid if His priorities become your own, you'll somehow lose something valuable? Are you afraid He won't make the best choice for you? Would you rather trust your command of the situation than His?

Usually we think this way when things are a mess, when our lives are just not working. It's when your world isn't cooperating, your husband is clueless, your kids are rebelling, and your future looks darker than the pit you're in. That's when we hold on even tighter, when we try to force everything and everyone into our ideas and *make* our lives work. Giving up just a bit of that grip we've got on everything is out of the question, so we get lost in the darkness and still try to find our own way out.

But God's way is different. He is light, and He knows best the paths we should take. All the chaos in our lives won't go away if we let that light in, but when our priority becomes following Him, we lose control and gain peace. We can say, "I don't have to be in charge because He is." And the fear is gone.

His Priorities

If we ignore the light our Shepherd wants to shine in our lives, we'll always regret it. Many years ago, I wanted to take a sign language class. I was completely intrigued with the idea. The class was going to be so convenient, offered just a mile or so from my home, and I was excited and as ready as a champagne cork on New Year's Eve. Until I told some of my family and friends, that is. Because of their reaction (they thought I was nuts) and because I couldn't come up with a good enough reason (to them) to take the class, I withdrew from it. I gave up, and I've regretted it ever since. There has never been the same opportunity for that class.

I wonder what blessings God had in store for me through that class, or what mission He had for me that I'm not qualified to do now. I'll never know. How could I refuse to serve Him by getting lost in my fears and letting a priority other than His guide me?

When we're lost, we're fighting God, and this kind of dark lostness is no exception. Only by letting His light in do we see our way out. Believing in that power means to preface our actions with the faith that He knows best and will always choose the best path for us.

Believing means letting Him lead us not *astray* but in *accord* with His purposes. Believing means being willing to overcome our fear in absolute certainty of the joy to come. Believing means we don't have to suffer in the darkness of lost priorities, because we know our Shepherd's first priority is finding us.

For Reflection

How have the priorities of fear and love of the wrong things led you into the darkness?

What has been more important to you than acting on your belief in Christ?

Does getting lost this way come easily to you?

What time in this darkness from long ago still hurts you today?

My Shepherd who sees in the dark, please help me overcome my fears that make me put anything in my life before You. Help my belief guide me to choose only the path You've created for me. Amen.

10

The Darkness of Lost Self-Control

Do not withhold your mercy from me, O LORD; may your love and
your truth always protect me. For troubles without number surround
me; my sins have overtaken me, and I cannot see.

Psalm 40:11–12

We all have lots of excuses when we get lost in this way. We lose
not the control over our lives but *self*-control. That leads us into a
painful darkness. David knew it well:

When Uriah's wife heard that her husband was dead, she mourned
for him. After the time of mourning was over, David had her brought
to his house, and she became his wife and bore him a son. But the
thing David had done displeased the LORD.

2 Samuel 11:26–27

King David let his lack of self-control override any sense of
right and wrong and all the good judgment he ever had. He stole
Uriah's wife and then had Uriah killed. That's a drastic example

of lost self-control. Even though we can learn a lot about pain and regret from that story, we still go the wrong way ourselves today.

We don't send an enemy into a battle that will lead to certain death, but sometimes we put our poor judgment front and center. We wander far away from the pasture God's provided to one that looks like a hundred-year drought in the making. And then we have to live there a while. We may be very sorry, like David, but we still have to journey back through the heavy darkness.

Lostness Repeated

Today this darkness for us may be a wrong action, as it was for David, or it may be a *lack* of action, such as not believing, not learning from our mistakes, not taking care of our hearts and souls. Our thoughts control us instead of us controlling them. And regardless of how this darkness manifests itself in our lives, and however many times we get lost this way, we know the valley well. The steps are always the same.

We rationalize our choices, we justify our behavior, and then we wonder where we were going in the first place. Whatever we thought we were seeking, it's not there now. There's no prize, no finish line, no peace. But there is hope.

God works with what we give Him, with the lives we have *today*. And everything we lose, He can restore to us. We can regain our self-control and escape the darkness when we realize that what we were looking for was something we'd let go of to begin with—our connection to our Shepherd.

We turned our backs on Him, didn't consult Him with our decisions, and then chose poor ways to deal with our feelings of inferiority. But when we are empowered instead of inferior, we ooze control that is *God's* control showing through us. When we feel inferior, we forget how precious we are to our Shepherd and start to gauge our worth by those around us. We always come up short and seek something to make us feel better that He wouldn't choose for us. No wonder we get lost!

We're running in the direction opposite where He wants us to go, choosing emptiness when so much bounty has been made for us. Like the whole nation of Israel God chastised and warned through Jeremiah, we are lost:

> "My people have committed two sins: They have forsaken me, the spring of living water, and have dug their own cisterns, broken cisterns that cannot hold water. . . . Have you not brought this on yourselves by forsaking the LORD your God when he led you in the way? . . . Consider then and realize how evil and bitter it is for you when you forsake the LORD your God and have no awe of me," declares the Lord, the LORD Almighty.
>
> Jeremiah 2:13, 17, 19

How many times do we choose the "broken cisterns," the inferior lives we make for ourselves, when the "living water" of our Shepherd's offering goes unused? Why do we complicate our lives that way?

Being the scattered sheep we are, we sometimes confuse God's peaceful pasture with one we think we can create for ourselves through our self-destructive behavior. But He knows our one-sided, self-filled view. He sees us grasp our way in the darkness, and despite what led us there, He knows the way out. He knows too how painful it may be for us, but He never says we're not worth guiding back to Him. Like David, our darkness doesn't have to last:

> Blessed is he whose transgressions are forgiven, whose sins are covered. Blessed is the man whose sin the LORD does not count against him and in whose spirit is no deceit.
>
> Psalm 32:1–2

When we feel connected to our Shepherd, we don't have to feel insignificant or lacking in anything. And then our question of *self*-control really isn't one. We simply hear our Shepherd's voice and align our will with His, nourished with the best He has to offer in

49

His living water. We give control of our self over to Him, and it isn't dark anymore.

For Reflection

How have you lost self-control by your actions or inactions?

What did you find with your self-filled choices?

What made you feel inferior as you wandered into this darkness?

> *My Shepherd who sees in the dark, please empower me with Your control of my life so that I don't choose my own misguided way. Help me feel Your hope for me as I hope for a way back to You. Amen.*

11

THE DARKNESS OF
LOST FORGIVENESS

For he has rescued us from the dominion of darkness and brought us
into the kingdom of the Son he loves, in whom we have redemption,
the forgiveness of sins.

Colossians 1:13–14

This is certainly one kind of lostness for which we are solely responsible. No one—absolutely no one—can forgive for us. We make
that choice completely of our own free will. That's great relief and
great responsibility.

Forgiving is one of the hardest things we usually do, and I don't
know which is harder: forgiving others or forgiving ourselves. Refusing either, though, creates a darkness that threatens to envelop
our whole world.

That's what happened to the servant Jesus told Peter about.
When the servant asked his master for mercy and patience to repay
his large debt, the master took pity on him and canceled the debt

altogether. But the servant failed to pass on the forgiveness. He encountered one of his own servants who owed him money and couldn't pay. Instead of showing the mercy shown him, the servant had his servant thrown into prison. His master found out and was stunned by his servant's behavior:

> In anger his master turned him over to the jailers to be tortured, until he should pay back all he owed. This is how my heavenly Father will treat each of you unless you forgive your brother from your heart.
>
> Matthew 18:34–35

That story still doesn't make it easy. It's tough to forgive others who hurt us or someone we love because the agony of the event is so real and deep. We can't separate the pain from the person who caused it, so every time we feel a hurt from whatever happened, we see that person's face. How can we forgive others when it's their fault we're hurting? How can we forgive ourselves if the face we associate with the pain is our own?

We walk in that darkness of lost forgiveness because we think forgiving means condoning, but it doesn't. And we sometimes think forgiving has to be quick and instant like everything else in our world, but it doesn't. We can look at how these misconceptions keep us in the dark by examining our own motives and timing and taking a cue from the Shepherd.

Motives. Sometimes we see no reason to forgive someone who's hurt us, because we know they don't deserve our forgiveness. And we certainly don't want to give them permission to forget what they did! No, we want to punish them, so we withhold any kind of pardon, even if that's contrary to our Shepherd's example.

Certainly God could say we don't deserve His forgiveness, and He'd be right. He could say we need to remember what we've done wrong, and He'd be right there too. But He looks past all that to get us out of the darkness.

His goal is not punishment but growth. Does that mean we don't face consequences for our actions? No, but those are a result of *our* choices, not God's. He's still there to work with what we give Him, and He wants all of us, even the ugly parts.

In our human relationships, we can help our hearts grow a little when we forgive, whether the person we forgive grows or not. When we look at ourselves instead of at those who hurt us, and we make our own learning and discovering a part of our motives, we make the forgiveness about ourselves and *our* journey, not about the pain or the person who caused it. We don't have to stay in the darkness.

When it's ourselves we're trying to forgive, the same reasoning applies. We often want to punish our own hearts the most when we've failed God, others, or ourselves. Do we deserve to forgive ourselves and forget what we've done? It doesn't matter, God says, because we may never feel we *deserve* forgiveness, but our need to grow and learn and discover has found a home in our willingness to forgive ourselves as well as others.

Even when we forgive, we still have a history that doesn't change. Yours might be one you don't want to revisit. That's fine; you don't have to. What's important is what comes next. When we focus on our hurt, no matter where it comes from, we're lost and separated from God. But He waits to help us with those hurts, to teach us to forgive by example, to rescue us, and to guide us toward the pasture He's planned.

Now if I make all that sound too simple and quick, I apologize. God may forgive with the blink of an eye, but it's not something that comes easily to most of us little sheep. We see forgiveness as a giant mountain we have to leap in one pious bound, but like most other things in our lives, it's a journey of climbing, not springing. Trying to hurry it will only endanger our steps.

Timing. I don't think God owns a watch. I think He wonders why we do. His timing is a mystery to us, and we aren't privy to how it works. We see the results, though, when we humbly and genuinely ask His forgiveness and know it's granted instantly because He promised. And then we know how far we are from operating on that same schedule.

God can breathe His forgiveness true and real and fast, but we don't know if we'll live long enough to find the same forgiveness in our hearts. That's a cold darkness because it adds pressure to our pain. We know we need to forgive, but today didn't feel any better than yesterday, and getting past the pain seems impossible. And maybe right now it is. Maybe your hurt is so deep no light can get to it yet. But don't give up. God's working.

Some people say time heals all wounds. I don't know if that's true, but giving yourself time to forgive allows God time to heal *you*. Remember, He's focusing on what remains, and He knows that within your broken heart is the life He planted—the vine that needs light to bloom—and He will restore it to you. Give Him time.

And give yourself time to recover, to receive before you try to give. When those hurts are big, your hill of forgiveness will look like Mount Saint Helens. Accept that. Know no little puff of wind from you will destroy it and no tiny step will scale it. But the Shepherd's grace will lift you over it when you're ready, because each breath without a ticking watch grants you a step out of the darkness.

It's up to us to grant the forgiveness we need in our lives, but we don't have to do it alone. The Shepherd has plenty of practice forgiving us, and He couples it with an all-encompassing love to teach us how to do the same.

For Reflection

How do you feel about the story Jesus told?

When have you ever been the unmerciful servant or treated yourself like his servant?

Why is forgiveness hard for you sometimes?

> *My Shepherd who sees in the dark, please make me*
> *like the merciful master in the story, for myself and*
> *those around me, so that I may reflect Your forgiving*
> *light. Amen.*

12

THE DARKNESS OF
LOST SECURITY

When the Midianite merchants came by, his brothers pulled Joseph
up out of the cistern and sold him for twenty shekels of silver to the
Ishmaelites, who took him to Egypt. . . . Then they got Joseph's robe,
slaughtered a goat and dipped the robe in the blood. They took the
ornamented robe back to their father. . . . He recognized it and said,
"It is my son's robe! Some ferocious animal has devoured him. Joseph
has surely been torn to pieces."

Genesis 37:28, 31–33

Joseph's brothers were jealous of him. That jealousy led to their
lost security, which in turn led them to throw him in a pit, fake his
death, and sell him into slavery. If they couldn't have what he did,
they'd get him out of their sight.

Our security in who we are in God's eyes is something we never
have to lose. He wants us to be secure as His children, regardless
of anything that's going on in our lives or what others do or have.
But when we compare our bounty to someone else's, we always

come up short, and we get deep into the darkness of lost security. And every step carries us farther away from the place we think we want to be. That's what happened to Saul.

You'd think that as the first king of Israel, Saul would have felt tremendous security and connection with God. But he let his own arrogance corrupt it:

> When Saul realized that the Lord was with David and that his daughter Michal loved David, Saul became still more afraid of him, and he remained his enemy the rest of his days.
>
> 1 Samuel 18:28–29

Saul was jealous of David, felt threatened by him, and tried to kill him several times. He was so jealous that he lost his own security in his relationship with God. And that led to more losses, more mistakes, and more darkness, to the point that Saul killed himself. He had given up hoping to be found.

Secure in Our Choice

Anytime we doubt our security in God's love, we're lost, and that makes us doubt our faith and His care. Sometimes it's easy to doubt when we're struggling with heavy mistakes or the weight of a life of disappointments. But we can never lose His presence.

God doesn't play favorites. He doesn't love you better than He loves me because of all you've done or your special talents or anything else. If I'm jealous of what I see in you, though, I'll become greedy and vindictive and cruel—not because of anything you've done to me, but because I don't like who I am without what you have. What I need to see is that you have a *relationship* with God—not special favor or more of His love and grace.

What you have is what I can have, because He wants that relationship with me too. God is the Shepherd of *all* our hearts, and I'm lost when I worry far too much about yours while my own is breaking. My goal is not to lessen your security but to recapture my own—trusting only in my Shepherd to honor *His* promises.

His Choice Too

Perhaps we banish ourselves away to a far and empty pasture with this kind of lostness, the way Joseph's brothers did to him. We're afraid of the very thing we crave. We wonder, *How can the God I've shunned and doubted hold me close? How will He respond to my entreaty, and how can I relinquish this safe distance I've created and believe He'll welcome me into His heart? What if I ask for that secure relationship and He refuses?*

This is the lostness that comes following a career setback, a breakup, a financial loss, or any fear of something over which you have no control—when your life seems to rest in other hands and you give them more power than God, when you believe that some circumstance or situation can defeat the plan He has for your life. It's the time when we cry, "But God, I'm doing my best and it's *still* not enough!" It's when we don't think God's watching us implode, or if He is, He must not care.

I remember this darkness once for two or three years in worry over my husband and his job. It was absolutely one hit after another, and the cold and darkness closed in on me until I thought surely I would be flattened by fear. But I wasn't. I was found instead by my Shepherd who never left my side. Some of my worries came to pass and some of them didn't, but finally I realized it didn't matter. My place in God's heart and His concern for my life weren't going to change even if everything else did. I didn't have to stay in the darkness. Security was my choice because it was His first.

Insecurity Interrupted

We never know how long we'll be in that place of fear, but it's never one second longer than we allow. God's offer remains open—

unique to you and me—to meet us in the dark. Security in God's care is not a group possession. We each have to be willing to fall backward and discover that God is there to catch us.

The circumstances won't change and the history won't change, but the sense of our place in them will change—we'll be secure in God's control and secure in our faith. We'll know He's going to catch us and hold us up no matter what happens.

We can focus on our separate journeys and see both the easy and the hard as part of our travels. Our roads are unique. I'd be permanently lost on your road, but on mine, the detours are temporary. My security in my Shepherd will always pave my way to the light.

Joseph's security in his relationship with God allowed him to forgive his brothers and even save them from a terrible famine in their homeland. Imagine what we can do when we claim our security the way Joseph did.

For Reflection

When and why have you let your jealousy or fear or disappointment destroy your security in God?

How far away was He—and His care—when you chose to ask for His touch on your life?

My Shepherd who sees in the dark, please anchor my security in You so deeply that I never doubt my place in Your heart. Help me see You instead of my fears. Amen.

13

THE DARKNESS OF LOST BLESSINGS

A certain man was preparing a great banquet and invited many guests. . . . But they all alike began to make excuses. The first said, "I have just bought a field, and I must go and see it. Please excuse me." Another said, "I have just bought five yoke of oxen, and I'm on my way to try them out. Please excuse me." . . . [The man said,] "I tell you, not one of those men who were invited will get a taste of my banquet."

Luke 14:16, 18–19, 24

Sure, we know we get lost when we do the *wrong* things, but sometimes we get just as lost when we think we're doing the *right* things.

If we neglect the banquet of the Lord—having His attention and giving Him ours—we're lost in an illusion of our own sufficiency. It's easy when things are going well to say, "Thanks, Lord. I'll call You if I need You." But just as important as our white-knuckled grasp of God when we're terrified is the banquet of His company when we're not.

Maybe we think we don't need to dine at His table when we have fields to tend and oxen to yoke. But the blessing of that interaction—not because we're scared but because we're *not*—is deep revelation and insight on our fields and oxen and everything else.

We learn much at the feast that prepares us for the difficult times. And in a state of eagerness and willingness and attentiveness, we learn more of His purpose in our pasture. We can worship without worry, give without asking for something in return, and be a sheep obediently answering her Shepherd's call.

Shifting Focus

When we're in the midst of a trauma, our focus is on *us*. Still, faithful God responds without a hitch, and yes, blessings of security and safety abound. But we miss the other blessings He so wants to give when we neglect the times *outside* the emergency—the ordinary times.

If we'll go to the banquet where our focus is on God instead of ourselves, He will reveal so much more. We'll be in awe of the absolute microscopic interest He has in our lives, how He sits down with us at the oddest and least important times just because we're there. We'll find these times of unhurried communion with Him become our prayers "continually" (1 Thess. 5:17) when we draw on His wisdom in even the minor moments of our travels. Unchosen or ignored, though, these beautiful interactions are gone like blossoms blown away by the wind.

The blessings of a closer relationship with our Shepherd are ours to accept, bulging with surprises, but when we refuse them, the darkness envelops us. And even though the fields and oxen are fine, we're lost because something is missing from our hearts—something designed especially for us, something we can never create on our own. We're lost because we choose not to find that bounty of blessings the Shepherd prepared.

Never Apart from the Banquet

Avoiding the darkness is not about time management but about *mind* management. When we segregate our fields and oxen from

God's banquet—when we divide our time with God from our time without God—we get lost.

He is the God of the parted sea and the flooded land. He is the God of the widow's mite and the sparrow's breath. And He is the God of your marriage and your career and your morning commute and your afternoon walk. He is the God of all your purposes, all your potential, and all your possibilities.

The blessing of His voice in the emergency is the power to save, and the blessing of His voice in the nonemergency is the power to soar. Yet we so often choose to ignore His voice. We lose our way in the mundane by not inviting our Shepherd to make it magical.

Be still, and know that I am God.

Psalm 46:10

When we think of God's blessings as big-ticket items that we're given only occasionally, we lose the joy and amazement of dining on His delicious goodness every moment. It's not a "be good to me by giving me what I want" kindness He offers, but a never-ending smorgasbord of life with Him so close and in tune with everything we do, because that's what He does.

If we miss that element of our Shepherd's touch, we're lost in a darkness where we think of Him only as a go-to guy when panic sets in. Preoccupied with our fields and oxen, we keep plowing in the wrong direction, and the banquet table gets farther and farther away. God sets it for us and offers to meet us there. We call it blessing. He calls it love.

For Reflection

Have you met God at the banquet He's prepared for you lately?

If so, what happened, and if not, why?

How have you ever quarantined His availability to the emergency room of your life?

What blessings have you missed?

> *My Shepherd who sees in the dark, please make a banquet for me. Please help me see Your eagerness to meet me in the middle of everything and open my eyes to the generous fill You provide without end. Amen.*

14

THE DARKNESS OF LOST PURPOSE

Prepare your minds for action; be self-controlled; set your hope fully on the grace to be given you.

1 Peter 1:13

You know this darkness—when you've tried so hard to make something work and it just won't. You've prayed and worked and studied and prayed some more, but what you hoped for still doesn't come. I wish I had a secret formula I could reveal that would get you where you want to be in an instant. I don't. We often have to wade through disappointment after disappointment to get where we're going.

We grow weary and lose heart, and in that darkness we lose the grip on all God has in store for us. The going is tough, so we don't go at all. We've lost our purpose because we've lost our will. But we're not made for that. We're not made to give up and allow ourselves to drift away from our Shepherd. We're not made for defeat. We just have to make a choice to give up or grow up.

Growing Purpose

We can overcome our fear and reluctance when we look at everything as something God can use. All of that darkness can become part of our purpose, folded into who we are to make us more open, understanding, wise, generous, gracious, forgiving—whatever our Shepherd needs us to be. Preparing for growth is the first step.

Or we can turn away from God and see the darkness as bigger than He is and follow it. Then we languish in the pasture where everything bad grows up around us while we let it overtake the fertile ground put there by our Shepherd.

But God's choice is to use it all as mulch. Sometimes we can't see it clearly, but it's happening. Something grows every day in our relationship with Him. It may be on the inside, where we're working with God on something just for us, or it may be on the outside, where others see and touch what He's directing in our lives. It's all part of His plan.

We can make it all mulch too when we're intimately involved with Him, taking gardening lessons every chance we get. When we do so, we're too close to Him to get lost, but when we don't— when we shrug our shoulders, hang our heads, and say, "What's the use?"—we're lost in a land without purpose. The promise of doing all things through Christ who gives us strength (see Phil. 4:13) seems useless when we see nothing worthwhile to do.

So when we give up, we stumble off the path He's guarding so closely, and what we could tend into something wonderful overgrows our hearts with darkness. A life that could be lived with the Master Gardener becomes one lived alone. And that is the scariest place of all.

> I myself will search for my sheep and look after them. As a shepherd looks after his scattered flock when he is with them, so will I look after my sheep. I will rescue them from all the places where they were scattered on a day of clouds and darkness.
>
> Ezekiel 34:11–12

For Reflection

When have you ever lost your purpose? Why?

What mulch have you left untended, hiding it instead of giving it to God to work with?

How alone do you feel when you've given up?

My Shepherd who sees in the dark, please help me prepare my mind for the purposes You've chosen for me. Help me not to give up but instead to grow up in the garden tended by You. Amen.

Part 3

ALONE

We all, like sheep, have gone astray, each of us has turned to his own way.

Isaiah 53:6

That's us, isn't it? Even if others are lost too, it's still a solitary darkness in which we wander. We all know how it feels to be lost, to be in pain and fear and feel so far from our Shepherd. We're fighting Him every step, trying to make ourselves right, then trying to fix all we've broken.

We try and we fail because the job is too big for us. But in our deep and scary darkness, we panic because we feel alone. And we realize that getting lost isn't our biggest fear; being apart from God is. How will we ever find Him again, and will He even let us?

We are so far away from where we started, so far from the first tiny misguided step that got us here. We're deep in pain and fear, and God seems a distant memory, a ghost of a Shepherd we used to claim for our own.

And who can we blame? It's our backs that are turned to our Lord, not His to us. We've allowed this separation, perhaps unintentionally at first, but still, if there's a chasm of darkness, we put it there. And it's so cold here all alone. We have plenty of time to think, time to reflect on what got us here.

We may feel shame or guilt or confusion or anger, but it all leads us to the same place—need. We're not meant to be alone, away from our Shepherd. We're not equipped to travel the treacherous landscape alone, depending on ourselves for wisdom. We're not designed for going our own way, because when we do—when we take that path God didn't plan—we learn quickly why it's so dark.

His guiding light is gone, and we need it back. Climbing out of that darkness can take us a long time because we often take painful detours in search of the light. That's always what happens when we go it alone.

But what remains is always the better way—to go with God and be alone no more. Why does it take us so long to remember that sometimes? Maybe it's because we forget where to look for help.

For Reflection

Why do you sometimes think God's abandoned you when you've gotten lost?

How do you deal with your feelings of aloneness and isolation?

My Shepherd who is never far away, please take away
this horrible feeling of being alone and without You.
Help me find the light quickly. Amen.

15

ALONE IN HIDING

Why, O LORD, do you stand far off? Why do you hide yourself in
times of trouble?

Psalm 10:1

When we feel alone, we look around and see if anybody's there, wondering if God's there in the dark. Is He too angry to come and help us? Does He delight in our lostness and say it serves us right to feel cold and alone? Does He hide behind our tears, watching us as we panic and try to search our way through the unfriendly territory?

No, God doesn't do any of those things, but like David we can feel an abandonment and separation from our Shepherd. We don't know how to get back to Him, and we aren't too sure He wants us back. Sometimes we don't know how to look for Him, and we're afraid to believe *He'll* come looking for *us*.

How long, O LORD? Will you forget me forever?
How long will you hide your face from me?
How long must I wrestle with my thoughts
and every day have sorrow in my heart?

Psalm 13:1–2

It can be easier to blame God for our aloneness, to blame Him for hiding and not reaching for us. We sometimes try to justify our choices a little while longer, or fight our own battles within our sad hearts, questioning His commitment to us and making our walk in the dark the result of His failure to show up when we asked.

We feel alone and as alien as snow on the equator, and then the darkness gets even deeper.

For Reflection

Have you ever felt God hiding from you, and how did you react?

Did you think He could ever really abandon you?

Where was He when you thought He was hiding?

My Shepherd who is never far away, please don't hide from me! Please forgive my crazy thoughts and show Yourself in my next heartbeat. Amen.

16

ALONE IN DENIAL

About an hour later another asserted, "Certainly this fellow was with [Jesus], for he is a Galilean." Peter replied, "Man, I don't know what you're talking about!" Just as he was speaking, the rooster crowed. The Lord turned and looked straight at Peter. Then Peter remembered the word the Lord had spoken to him: "Before the rooster crows today, you will disown me three times." And he went outside and wept bitterly.

Luke 22:59–62

Sometimes it feels like it's not God hiding but us. Can you imagine how Peter must have felt when he lied and denied his Shepherd? Peter's denial may have seemed easier at the time, part of his insecurity or fear around those who might judge him. So he walked into a darkness that separated him from Christ, and he must have never felt so alone.

And when have we done the same? Perhaps we've not been in such a traumatic situation as Peter was, but we've surely felt alone when we denied God's power to heal and restore others or ourselves.

Maybe we've denied that He is the giver and forgiver of all, that He still works miracles today. Maybe we've turned our backs on His teachings and taken the easy way out, led by our insecurity or fear of those who might judge us.

Then when all of those people are gone, we are left alone with our choices, feeling separated from our Shepherd. Will He still come looking for us—or have we hurt Him with our selfish actions?

The pain is intense and we're alone in its depth and darkness. How did Peter ever find his way out?

For Reflection

When have you found yourself alone in denial?

What led you there, and how will you guard against it in the future?

> *My Shepherd who is never far away, please don't ever*
> *let me deny Your great love and presence in my life.*
> *I am nothing without You close to me, claiming me.*
> *Amen.*

17

ALONE IN SORROW

Be merciful to me, O LORD, for I am in distress; my eyes grow weak
with sorrow, my soul and my body with grief. My life is consumed
by anguish and my years by groaning; my strength fails because of
my affliction, and my bones grow weak.

Psalm 31:9–10

Sometimes we just hurt all over, inside and out. We can't think beyond our pain, and the silence of our hearts beating without God
seems louder than our cries. Where is He? We need Him, yet it feels
like He's denying us. And He probably has every right to, every
reason to watch us writhe in the bed we made—it's not His fault
we're here in the darkness. Now we're hurting too much to open
our eyes even a tiny bit to see if any light will shine on us again.

A deep depression consumes us, and we give up hope for a
while. Why bother? Everything we touch falls apart, and nobody
cares. We see no miracles coming for us, and we don't know how
to find our way without falling into more potholes. Can we do
nothing right? We identify with Job a little bit: "Yet when I hoped

for good, evil came; when I looked for light, then came darkness. The churning inside me never stops; days of suffering confront me" (Job 30:26–27).

Feeling abandoned and forsaken, we collapse into our pain, wondering if our Shepherd will even miss us or hear our cries if we call for Him. Is He still here? Could He come for us if He wanted? Would He? We wonder if Job or Peter had the same doubts.

For Reflection

When have you known that desperate aloneness of sorrow?

How have you felt like Job? If so, how did you respond?

> *My Shepherd who is never far away, please relieve me of this great sorrow in feeling alone without You. Help me see beyond this pain to You, surely still here with me, now and always. Amen.*

18

ALONE IN DOUBT

My God, my God, why have you forsaken me? Why are you so far
from saving me, so far from the words of my groaning?

Psalm 22:1

Oh, this is scary. When God is angry with us, we can hope for His
mercy. When He's teaching us, we can be grateful for His patience.
But when we can't find Him at all and He seems to have abandoned
us, we don't know what to do. He's in charge, and if He wants to
leave us in the dark, He certainly has the power to do it.

And what if He does? What if He decides we're not worth the
trouble of rescuing, that we're too wayward and worthless for His
pasture? That's probably how the son who left his father and squan-
dered his money felt. He wanted to return, but he didn't know
what he'd find:

"I will set out and go back to my father and say to him: Father, I have
sinned against heaven and against you. I am no longer worthy to be
called your son; make me like one of your hired men." . . . But while he
was still a long way off, his father saw him and was filled with compassion for him . . . [and said,] "Let's have a feast and celebrate."

Luke 15:18–20, 23

Does our Father see us when we're "still a long way off"? We don't know. That feeling is the deepest pain, the fear of having to go through this world without our Shepherd, the feeling of being forever lost and alone and knowing it's His choice to leave us in that state. Will He ignore us, or will He celebrate our return? Will He refuse to answer our cries and reject our pleas for His presence?

It could happen, we fear. Because our own faithfulness and grace is often lacking, we doubt the Lord's promises too, especially since we've separated ourselves from Him and chosen the wrong way. So what do we do when we're alone and afraid we'll always be this way? Will He answer if we call from the darkness? Will He relieve our heavy hearts and guide us back to Himself?

There's only one way to find out. And desperately we seek Him.

In my alarm I said, "I am cut off from your sight!" Yet you heard my cry for mercy, when I called to you for help.

Psalm 31:22

For Reflection

What experiences have made you doubt whether God would accept you when you asked Him to?

How many times have you wondered whether He's given up on you?

How has that fear kept you feeling alone even longer?

My Shepherd who is never far away, please prove my fears wrong! Welcome me back by Your grace and celebrate our closeness. Please keep Your promise to me. Amen.

19

ALONE IN REPENTANCE

I have strayed like a lost sheep. Seek your servant, for I have not forgotten your commands.

Psalm 119:176

In our despair, we put our doubts up against God's faithfulness and see which one comes out on top. Our Shepherd will never fail to answer us, and He responds when our repentant hearts cry. We can't ask Him to lead us and then want to chart the course ourselves, though.

Only by submitting to His wisdom (which, if we were smarter sheep, we would have done in the beginning) do we feel ourselves moving closer to Him again. We realize we are the ones who have wandered, because He can never go away from us, even when we're being a bit difficult. We finally realize we feel alone and abandoned only because we allow it, never because He dictates it.

No matter how full of regret or shame or guilt we are, it's never so much that God would choose to leave us in the darkness of our pain. A plea from the heart is all He needs to flood us with the light of His grace. "'Return to me,' declares the LORD Almighty, 'and I will return to you'" (Zech. 1:3).

Then it's up to us to choose a path to follow, a garden to grow. The dizzy little sheep needs a contrite heart ready to bloom and a commitment to walk with her Shepherd. And that means a step out in constant surrender to her Lord. Looking for the light comes with every breath. "If you repent, I will restore you that you may serve me" (Jer. 15:19).

For Reflection

What caused your feelings of aloneness in the past?

How big was your regret or shame or guilt in the light of God's grace?

Was it big enough to keep God from you, from wanting to be with you?

My Shepherd who is never far away, please accept my plea and know my heart. Help me remember which one of us always creates the divide—and what makes it disappear. Amen.

20

ALONE IN PRAYER

Hear my voice when I call, O LORD; be merciful to me and answer me. My heart says of you, "Seek his face!" Your face, LORD, I will seek. Do not hide your face from me, do not turn your servant away in anger; you have been my helper. Do not reject me or forsake me, O God my Savior.

Psalm 27:7–9

Our Shepherd *is* here! We don't have to face the darkness alone. We begin to believe His promise, and we pray. Then we pray some more. We pray in the dark and know His face will guide us from our misguided steps. We ask Him not to hide, not to be angry, not to abandon us. We're still hurting, still feeling lost, but we're reaching out in trust instead of doubt. Somehow that makes all the difference.

We pray in words and we pray in tears. We pray in cries and we pray in silence. We sometimes feel so confused or sad that we don't know how to pray. But no special form or protocol is required—only the belief in our Shepherd's promise to hear and answer. So we pray some more, the best we can, and His own efforts meet ours:

> The Spirit helps us in our weakness. We do not know what we ought to pray for, but the Spirit himself intercedes for us with groans that words cannot express.
>
> Romans 8:26

We discover in all the time we've felt alone that we haven't been even a blink away from our Father's sight. He has followed us into our darkness and knows our anguish well. His own is probably just as great as He waits for us to pray in whatever way we can, to trust Him once again with our ragged fears so that He can plan a rescue.

Our prayers that seem so desperate at first become a great comfort, as we know in our hearts they are being heard. We are never alone, and through our prayers we become aware of just how close our Shepherd is—close enough to touch, committed enough to find us.

> My eyes are ever on the LORD, for only he will release my feet from the snare.
>
> Psalm 25:15

For Reflection

How do your prayers comfort you when you feel alone?

How does God make His close presence known to you?

> *My Shepherd who is never far away, please hear my prayers. Walk with me and talk with me and hear my praise and my pleas from the darkness. Amen.*

21

ALONE IN RESCUE

Then you will call, and the LORD will answer; you will cry for help, and he will say: Here am I.

Isaiah 58:9

Our Shepherd always answers. We doubt and we wonder how and we're afraid to hope, but He does, because He's in pain too when we're feeling alone. He knows that apart from Him we can do nothing but cry, feel nothing but despair, and see nothing but darkness.

And knowing we can't find our own path to the lighted pasture, He makes us one. It's always one step behind Him, so we hold His hand and trust His lead.

Then we know we're not alone. The land we travel may look rocky and unforgiving, but it doesn't matter because we don't walk it alone. The terrain hasn't changed, but we have—we have cried out in both despair and hope and our Shepherd has answered and hugged us to His heart.

"Here I am," He says, tapping us gently on the shoulder to remind us He was never *not* here. All those feelings of abandonment and rejection and doubt evaporate because He has rescued us from them and from ourselves.

It's our responsibility to ask for God's rescue from the darkness, and it's His promise and pleasure to respond. We don't hide and neither does He.

> I trust in you, O LORD; I say, "You are my God." My times are in your hands. . . . Let your face shine on your servant; save me in your unfailing love.
>
> Psalm 31:14–16

He can't let go of us, and we are forever connected to Him. Yes, we wander off and lose our way, but He still calls us His own and will not rest until we are found, no matter what it takes.

For Reflection

How do you feel in that moment before God rescues you?

How do you feel when He taps your shoulder and you look to see Him there?

> *My Shepherd who is never far away, please help me*
> *see You always close, always here, never leaving me.*
> *Rescue me and hug me tight. Amen.*

Part 4

FOUND

We are his people, the sheep of his pasture.

Psalm 100:3

The lost son, the lost sheep, the lost you and me—all feeling alone, all afraid, but all loved more than we can understand. Our Shepherd has stayed with us as we've wandered astray, has heard us cry, and has seen us fail to save ourselves. We finally see our only hope for a rescue, our only light in the darkness.

For reasons we can't explain and barely dare to consider, our Shepherd won't leave us lost and feeling alone. He finds us every time, and beyond that, He leads us to a home full of blessings with many more to come, a home even better than the one we left.

Finding Me

He did it. Steeped in His power and true to His promise, my Shepherd found me and rescued me from the cold darkness. How did He do that? How did He know exactly what I needed and how to reach for me at exactly the right moment? And perhaps more important, why? Why would He devote such time and energy to *me*, the little nearsighted sheep with a map-reading disability?

Maybe He knows something I don't. Maybe His patience is exceeded only by His love and detective skills and He's not done with me yet. I believe it's true—He does know the hidden pastures better than I do, and nothing will give Him greater pleasure than to guide me through them, to be both partner and leader in my life.

Always Looking, Always Knowing

We don't know how long the shepherd in Jesus' story searched for his lost sheep. Did anyone tell him he was wasting his time? Did anyone think he should forget about the troublemaker? Does God ever think that about His lost sheep? He doesn't.

As insignificant as I seem in the grand scheme of things, *He* came looking for *me*. He wanted me back, regardless of my missteps and refusals to listen. He wanted me back enough to rescue me from the dark pit I'd crawled into. He always does. And like a stubborn child who's tired of struggling, I want Him to want me back, as I'm amazed at His love and patience. I want Him to be right. I finally stop shaking my head and demanding my way and relax into His ever-faithful heart.

Then I squeal with joy as He lifts me onto His shoulders like the shepherd in the story who is so relieved his sheep is safe again. I throw my head back and breathe in the love that brought Him to me. And the reunion begins, because He knows something I don't.

> You are a shield around me, O LORD; you bestow glory on me and lift up my head. To the LORD I cry aloud, and he answers me from his holy hill.
>
> Psalm 3:3–4

From His position, with the whole view of my world, He sees all the travels to come that I can only guess about. He sees me in the places He's already chosen and prepared, yet He waits for me to follow Him there. He knows my flaws and all the detours I can take, but He sees beyond all that to the journey and the joy our travels together can be. And because He finds me, I can see what He sees too.

I can know a bit of what He knows, and I don't have to feel lost and alone again. There must be something so wonderful, so special, so worthwhile still to come—why else would He seek me and find me without fail? Surely there are less ornery sheep to corral. But I'll leave that decision to Him and look to see what He still sees in me, His weak and imperfect sheep in tattered fur.

> I have seen his ways, but I will heal him;
> I will guide him and restore comfort to him.
>
> Isaiah 57:18

Maybe He's nearsighted too, because the mess I'm in seems of little concern to Him. "Look," He rejoices, "I've found her!" I only see His happiness as He withholds the commentary on my condition and focuses on my presence in His arms. Maybe that's His practice. Maybe He'll explain it to me.

For Reflection

When has your Shepherd found you, and how did the reunion feel?

What has He revealed to you about your travels to come?

My Shepherd who finds me, thank You! Please show me everything that's possible because I never gave up and neither did You. Amen.

22

FOUND TO BE GUIDED

For you were like sheep going astray, but now you have returned to the Shepherd and Overseer of your souls.

1 Peter 2:25

Our Shepherd is always three steps ahead of us in His planning and rescuing. He finds us because He promised He always would, and then He says, "There's more. Don't stay here in the dark. Let Me guide you out."

And He offers more—to oversee our whole lives, always knowing better for us than we know ourselves. Will we follow Him and trust Him to deliver what He says He can, to give us more? It's a big production with Him—because the reunion is a new start for Him too, a new chance to be that part of our lives He so wants to be, a chance to live out His love and grace through us, a chance to guide us where we've been afraid to go before.

Sometimes we may think being found is the end of some bad choices, but God says it's the beginning of bigger choices. We think being found is the brightest picture of our Shepherd's love, and while it is dramatic, the guidance He provides after is blinding with its light. The elation and gratitude we feel at being found doesn't have to end. It can deepen instead of fade when we choose to follow our Guide, learning with each step.

He is both teacher and rescuer when we stumble. He doesn't waste His time finding us only to let us fail to recognize how we got lost. He is never short of mercy and never reluctant to pair it with instruction.

A Constant Guide

In the story of the woman caught in adultery and brought before those gathered to learn from Jesus, we see an example of His desire to guide us not just once but always. Those who had brought the woman there couldn't condemn her when Jesus showed them that their own lives were lived in the dark:

> "Neither do I condemn you," Jesus declared. "Go now and leave your life of sin."
> When Jesus spoke again to the people, he said, "I am the light of the world. Whoever follows me will never walk in darkness, but will have the light of life."
>
> John 8:11–12

Our Shepherd knows we're not up to facing the challenges of this world alone. Do you think His grace left that woman, or do you think He spoke to her in her heart forever after to lead her in the way He chose? She was given a priceless gift in His lack of condemnation, and then He matched it with His gift of guidance. The light He's planned for us awaits our acceptance of those gifts too, our choice to stop fighting and start following. But we need to know how.

Choosing to Follow

Peter and John traveled together healing and preaching God's Word. Their enthusiasm and their message angered and frightened the Sadducees who didn't believe in Jesus' resurrection. They asked Peter and John by whose authority they spoke, and Peter answered that it was by the Shepherd Christ:

> When they saw the courage of Peter and John and realized that they were unschooled, ordinary men, they were astonished and they took note that these men had been with Jesus.
>
> Acts 4:13

We may be quite unschooled and ordinary when God finds us, maybe even a bit low on the learning curve, but that changes when He pulls us to Him and says, "Let's go." We can't follow Him if we refuse to be guided. He's made His choice out of mercy for our weak souls, and it's up to us to make ours.

Peter and John chose to follow, to be brave and unafraid because they knew their Shepherd was in charge and deserving of their devotion. They needed no degrees or titles to make their choice—just a willingness to be led as He saw fit. "My sheep listen to my voice; I know them, and they follow me" (John 10:27).

May we follow our Shepherd and say as Jesus did, "The one who sent me is with me; he has not left me alone, for I always do what pleases him" (John 8:29). Knowing we will be forever guided by our Shepherd, may we make ourselves available not only in gratitude but also in obedience, beginning where we are found.

May those who see our walk take note that we've "been with Jesus" too.

For Reflection

How do you accept your Shepherd's guidance, trusting He knows best?

What do you do that causes people to note you've "been with Jesus"?

My Shepherd who finds me, please help me see the value of the gift of Your guidance. Let my every step be made because I've been with You. Amen.

23

FOUND JUST AS WE ARE

This is what the LORD says: "As when juice is still found in a cluster
of grapes and men say, 'Don't destroy it, there is yet some good in
it,' so will I do in behalf of my servants."

Isaiah 65:8

Every time my Shepherd has found me, He's hugged me to Him
right then with arms open wide, encircling all my fears and doubts
and turning them to nothing with the power of His squeeze. I can't
remember Him ever saying, with a palm outstretched like a traffic
cop, "Wait! Come to Me when you've got something worthy to
show Me. Grow up by yourself." Never has that happened. And
it never will.

Like whitewash on a fence, the Lord's grace covers us, and we
only need make ourselves still and accepting, because just as we
are is how He works best. Trying to make ourselves into something
we're not yet is still resistance, like a stiff-armed child in the grip
of a parent, afraid of what God has in store. No, we're found just
as we are for a reason.

Our Shepherd isn't afraid of our condition because it becomes part of His plan. He finds us in our needy, vastly imperfect states not because we deserve it, but because He wants to find us that way. It's how He works best. Paul understood that:

> I am the least of the apostles and do not even deserve to be called an apostle, because I persecuted the church of God. But by the grace of God I am what I am, and his grace to me was not without effect.
>
> 1 Corinthians 15:9–10

About as lost as a sheep can get, Paul began his journey blind and without a map, no doubt wondering what his part in the Lord's plan would be. He couldn't change what had happened, and God didn't expect him to. He found Paul just as he was and began there. Being found always begets a new beginning.

Again, the story of the lost son reminds us of ourselves, our own fears—wanting to go home to God but afraid of His reaction. When the way we are is so far from the way we want to be, we feel unworthy to even ask for forgiveness and rescue.

But again, our Father sees something we don't. He sees from that high place where the paths are clear—and our path still remains. It has been waiting for us, and our Shepherd and Guide sees beyond our sorry appearance, not to how we are but to how we can be. He sees a reason to rejoice, as did the father in the story. He sees the reunion first and only. "This son of mine was dead and is alive again; he was lost and is found" (Luke 15:24).

The found son, found sheep, found you and me—none of us looks much like the cover of a magazine after our time in the dark. But the Shepherd never mentions that. He just focuses on the celebration. So can we.

For Reflection

What shape have you been in when your Shepherd has found you?

How did that change His acceptance of you?

> *My Shepherd who finds me, thank You for Your willingness to find me as I am. Please help me always see that willingness and never destroy any of my grapes that might make juice. Amen.*

24

FOUND READY OR NOT

I have considered my ways and have turned my steps to your statues.
I will hasten and not delay to obey your commands.

                                                          Psalm 119:59–60

Sometimes we get so used to our lostness that we're almost too afraid
to be found, and we settle for waiting until we're more prepared,
until we understand more and have more to offer our Shepherd in
return for His search. We behave as if we control the script of our
rescue. God knows when it's time, when our cry is perfect, and when
the reunion can wait no longer. Sometimes we're not so sure.

Perhaps Paul was far from ready—at least in his thinking—but
the Lord had other plans. "Who are you, Lord?" he asked the voice
from the light (Acts 9:5). Clearly Paul wasn't expecting a rescue. And
neither was Ananias. We sometimes overlook the doubt Ananias
was lost in because of the dramatic story of Paul. And we can still
display the same tendency to argue that Ananias did. The Lord told
him to find Paul and restore his sight (see Acts 9:10–12):

"Lord," Ananias answered, "I have heard many reports about this man and all the harm he has done to your saints in Jerusalem. . . ." But the Lord said to Ananias, "Go!"

Acts 9:13, 15

Whether we think we're ready or not to move on God's plans, *He* knows. He defies all limited, human logic—such as choosing the Christians' chief opponent to become a chief disciple—and what He decides will prevail, because He never sets a goal and then realizes He has no tools with which to accomplish it.

Granted, His talent is considerable given that He has to work with what we provide, but that doesn't seem to matter. His grace accompanies His orders, and getting to be part of His work is one of the most wonderful blessings reserved for those who accept His hand in challenge. We can trust we're ready when He says "Go!" even when our human fears try to tell us we're not.

God finds us for His grand reasons when we're willing to learn how to follow. Sure, we may get lost again, still living in our less-than-perfect skin, but we'll have a better understanding of the path before us. Maybe we'll even see that *being* ready means *learning how* to be ready when He says it's time for one of our purposes to come to light. "The day for building your walls will come, the day for extending your boundaries" (Micah 7:11).

We are found so we can prepare, so we can grow our trust and believe that the Shepherd-guided "building" and "extending" will come when He has made us ready. We just have to be ready for our rescue, and He leads us the rest of the way.

For Reflection

How ready are you for God's next grand purpose?

Are you willing to learn how to be ready?

What are you afraid of, and what are your questions for your Shepherd?

> *My Shepherd who finds me, please forgive my reluctance to follow. I'm sometimes afraid and sometimes a little stubborn, but I trust You can and will make me ready for anything You choose. Amen.*

25

FOUND NO MATTER HOW LOST

May the God of hope fill you with all joy and peace as you trust in him,
so that you may overflow with hope by the power of the Holy Spirit.

Romans 15:13

There is no place dark enough to keep the Shepherd away. He isn't afraid of where He'll have to go to find us, what misbeliefs He'll have to correct, or what mistakes He'll have to forgive. We cannot get too lost for His radar, but sometimes we think we can get too lost for His grace to do anything with us.

Maybe we've been astray too long for Him to care anymore. Maybe He's rethought that grace thing and it's not perfect or powerful enough for us anymore. Maybe we can figure things out on our own if we just try a little longer and let God bless the deserving people, those who seem less lost. Who are we that He should wade into the darkness of our souls and breathe His light?

Yet He says we're His. "You are a chosen people . . . belonging to God, that you may declare the praises of him who called you out of darkness into his wonderful light" (1 Peter 2:9).

His Choice

The equation depends not on our abilities or intellect but on God the Shepherd's faithfulness. His decision never wavers. His sense of direction never falters even when we don't make the hunt easy.

Sometimes we almost give up hope when we see little reason to rejoice or trust in what lies ahead. Maybe we've suffered such hurts that it's easier to give up, and we crawl into a dark hole where we wallow in emptiness. Every day is darker than the last, and being lost feels normal, being alone expected. But our Shepherd hasn't walked away! He hasn't given up hope, and He will restore ours to us in one breath and give our lives the light they need.

I wonder if Peter lost hope, if he saw the life he'd planned with Jesus disappearing after his doubts and denials of his Savior. Jesus died an earthly death before Peter was found, but a darkness, a grave, and a resurrection led to a powerful reunion and purposeful future:

> Again Jesus said, "Simon son of John, do you truly love me?" He answered, "Yes, Lord, you know that I love you." Jesus said, "Take care of my sheep."
>
> John 21:16

Not only does He find us no matter how lost we are, but He also gives us a job to do. He found Peter in his darkest moment and restored him to the place He'd planned long before (see Matt. 16:18). There's no reason to believe His inclination has changed. Even when we don't know how to look for Him, He finds us anyway.

Beyond Hope

We can always hope, and we can be sure that our Shepherd will travel heaven and earth to bring us back to Him. I've been almost too lost to hope myself sometimes, afraid He wouldn't hear me cry or, worse, wouldn't answer if He did. *Why should He?* I reasoned. I had crawled away to a place I hated, but I didn't know how to get out. I decided the Lord would be just fine with leaving me there, and I prepared to stay in the dark, alone.

But *He* didn't give up hope. He didn't worry about the long trek I'd have to make to understand about His grace and His plans. He didn't care how rocky the terrain might get or how scatterbrained I'd be in my attempts to follow His directions.

He only cared that I answered when He called my name. No matter how lost I was, the Shepherd knew the way because He had planned for me a better path that I could choose despite my detours. He stood there with so much more, and I'm blessed to have my work as part of it.

His grace is too big for me to keep to myself. It's too big for you too. The reunion is the beginning of a life divinely planned. Our Shepherd knew it all along in Peter's case, and He knows it in ours.

For Reflection

When have you lost hope, so sure you were too lost to be found?

What were God's thoughts on your worries?

How did you respond to His hope in you?

> *My Shepherd who finds me, please help me see where*
> *I am, that it's never too far lost for You to find me.*
> *Help me hope for You while You hope for me, and let*
> *me know the joy of being part of Your plan. Amen.*

26

FOUND TO LOOK FOR OTHERS

So whether you eat or drink or whatever you do, do it all for the glory of God.

1 Corinthians 10:31

Of course we all appreciate great teachers and respond to their messages of faith in Christ. But what we often respond to even more is the touch of a friend, a hand extended to us that has touched the hand of God. And our Lord knows that, so He finds and makes ready those who can live for us the life of a follower of Christ.

We read about Apollos who originally "knew only the baptism of John" (Acts 18:25), but he studied and prepared and kept telling his story so that others might believe. I don't know if he was ever afraid or hesitant, but we can take him as a bold example of one of God's great purposes for us all:

When Apollos wanted to go to Achaia, the brothers encouraged him and . . . he was a great help to those who by grace had believed. For he vigorously refuted the Jews in public debate, proving from the Scriptures that Jesus was the Christ.

Acts 18:27–28

In what we might consider little ways, our Shepherd may be lead-ing us to look for others who are lost. Our words or choices may be the signs some other lost sheep needs to hear or see. Our reunion is too great a bounty to horde to ourselves! Authentic testimony will overflow if we allow it to. And that personal revelation touches more than we may ever know.

A Sheep Others Follow

So many of those we encounter every day are lost one way or another. And we don't have to look far to find someone who's trav-eled the same misguided path we have. By example, sometimes a deeply painful example, we learn a better way, a more secure path. And while we can't choose for someone else where and how she'll travel, we can be a beacon to light her way.

But, you may ask, what if someone doesn't ask for or want my advice? That doesn't matter because the path you're walking *now* is a living example of the Shepherd's grace poured out on you. You don't have to package that example in advice and instruction if she doesn't ask, but you can trust that your travels through the lost and found speak loudly anyway.

It's a matter of creating the "I want that too" effect—when your life is such a walk with God that others want to follow you. Being found by God and following Him creates in you something nothing else can—a peace and joy that shine no matter what, a way of approaching life with a ready-or-not attitude because you trust *God* is always ready.

Found by the Lost

Looking for others who may be lost is more about making our-selves available to be found by them than pursuing them. Think about your daily routine encounters as opportunities to demonstrate God's love and reflect His grace. We all have chances to do that every day in how we handle difficult situations, how we deal with criticism or disappointment, and how we respond when God says, "Go!"

In every meeting you have with a wayward soul, show that you understand—you've been there, so you know. Maybe your interaction with the lost sheep won't be big, but the bit of your life she lives with you might be just right for revealing what God's put there for her too. And your own journey will be even more richly blessed, for we cannot give without receiving when we give a little of the light our Shepherd has shined on us.

The best way to look for others is to be what they're looking for in themselves.

For Reflection

How has following a found sheep helped you before?

How have you been the sheep to follow?

What experience has helped you most recently create the "I want that too" effect for others?

My Shepherd who finds me, it's amazing You can take me and make me a sheep others can follow. Please help me find those who are lost and be an example of Your rescuing love and grace. Amen.

27

FOUND FOR REJOICING

The LORD your God is with you, he is mighty to save. He will take great delight in you, he will quiet you with his love, he will rejoice over you with singing.

Zephaniah 3:17

Even before we understand all that being found means in our lives, and certainly before we're able to translate our rescue into part of His plan for us, our Shepherd is pleased to hold us close. It's enough that we're with Him again. The shepherd in Jesus' story doesn't say, "Tell me, little sheep, how you'll make up for all this time and effort I've spent looking for you and how you'll repay my kindness." No, instead "he joyfully puts it on his shoulders and goes home. Then he calls his friends and neighbors together and says, 'Rejoice with me; I have found my lost sheep'" (Luke 15:5–6).

And our Shepherd does the same. He doesn't meet us with a list of chores to complete or demand restitution for His rescue. He joyfully lifts us up and carries us home to His heart, where the joy overflows.

Perhaps we're not such a great find—but it doesn't seem to matter because our Shepherd looks at our willingness to be found. Despite how long it might have taken or how many times He may have rescued us before, He finds joy in our recovery. We have to wonder why.

Rejoicing over Me

Rejoicing begets restarting—a fresh beginning is here and all possibilities are like new. God sees the new beginning in us and knows that our hearts and minds are surrendered to His hands. When we are found, we've stopped fighting, questioning, and disbelieving and moved on to living, breathing, and growing in the new place He's lifted us to. There our fear and resistance are replaced by joy and acceptance.

He rejoices when He finds us not because our condition is so great but because He's ready to change it, and so are we. And then we see the possibilities He's arranged for us, and He sees our joy in return.

> I delight greatly in the LORD; my soul rejoices in my God. For he has clothed me with garments of salvation and arrayed me in a robe of righteousness.
>
> Isaiah 61:10

We might wonder why God would be so devoted to one of His troublesome sheep anyway. You'd think He would choose to do all His rejoicing and clothing over those not so difficult to find. What's one lost and never-found sheep anyway in the whole pasture of others? Apparently it's a lot, and it must not be neglected.

He can't *not* honor His Word, His promise of a rescue. Only found can we begin the new beginning. Only found can we carry on in our story. Only found can we know forever "the oil of gladness instead of mourning, and a garment of praise instead of a spirit of despair" (Isa. 61:3).

For Reflection

How does it feel to know the Lord takes great delight in you?

How do you respond to His joy with your own?

How do others see His joy in you?

> *My Shepherd who finds me, please rejoice with me, Your little sheep lost no more! Please help me celebrate our new beginning without questioning Your devotion but growing in it instead. Amen.*

28

FOUND BECAUSE HE PROMISED

I will never leave you nor forsake you.

Joshua 1:5

We're found because God never gives up on something He started. It's not in His nature to accept defeat and alter His plans because one of His sheep doesn't travel as scheduled. The "hope and a future" (Jer. 29:11) our Shepherd has prepared for us will not disintegrate or evaporate; it's waiting on us right now.

He promises a rescue when we ask:

"You will call upon me and come and pray to me, and I will listen to you. You will seek me and find me when you seek me with all your heart. I will be found by you," declares the LORD, "and will bring you back from captivity."

Jeremiah 29:12–14

The "captivity" we're lost in can be anything, such as what we've discussed so far, but it's always of our own making. The darkness tries to win and keep us there, separated and alone, but God says He has not forsaken us. He's working in us the whole time, preparing for the reunion He both orchestrates and allows:

> I will give them a heart to know me, that I am the LORD. They will be my people, and I will be their God, for they will return to me with all their heart.

Jeremiah 24:7

Sure, we fear that He could deny us, hide from us, abandon us. But He won't. He'd much rather walk *with* us while His miracles delight and amaze us every day. The miracles become the essence of our lives, evidence of a faith not denied.

And we have plenty of evidence of God's faithfulness to His promises. Stephen, "a man full of God's grace and power" (Acts 6:8), spoke about the kingdom of Christ to all who would listen. In a speech before the Sanhedrin, a court of Jews who ruled over religious affairs in Israel, he began with a promise of God:

> So [Abraham] left the land of the Chaldeans and settled in Haran. After the death of his father, God sent him to this land where you are now living. He gave him no inheritance here, not even a foot of ground. But God promised him that he and his descendants after him would possess the land, even though at that time Abraham had no child.

Acts 7:4–5

And so it came to be. What seemed impossible to Abraham wasn't, because God promised and delivered. What seems impossible to us so often today—our rescue and redemption—isn't, because God promises and will deliver.

Jesus said, "The Son of Man came to seek and to save what was lost" (Luke 19:10). That's me. That's you. And because our Shepherd always does what He promises, we are redeemed and recovered, made ready for our own lives of miracles.

Nothing Too Hard

God spoke through Judah's prophet Isaiah about His ability and inclination to grow and create from unlikely sources. And who could be more unlikely a repository of possibilities than a hardheaded sheep lost from her Shepherd?

> Sharon will become a pasture for flocks, and the Valley of Achor a resting place for herds, for my people who seek me.
>
> Isaiah 65:10

From a swamp near the Mediterranean Sea (Sharon) and a desert near the Dead Sea (Achor), God promised a fertile valley. It's the same with us—His promise is our potential, His redemption our renaissance. Becoming part of His plan is our blessing, the journey a joy.

I don't know why He likes to stack the deck against Himself and choose the most inferior and faulty tools to work His miracles with—tools like me—but He does. Perhaps as Paul discovered, our awareness of His abilities and choices is part of our rescue. Paul told the Christians in Corinth about his and Timothy's difficult time in Asia, where perhaps they gave in to the darkness, allowing their hearts to hurt and dare to doubt if their Shepherd was still with them:

> We do not want you to be uninformed, brothers, about the hardships we suffered in the province of Asia. We were under great pressure, far beyond our ability to endure, so that we despaired even of life. Indeed, in our hearts we felt the sentence of death. But this happened that we might not rely on ourselves but on God, who raises the dead.
>
> 2 Corinthians 1:8–9

We know Paul's feelings of "beyond our ability" when we're lost too. We feel dead to God's love and promises, cut off from His sight and too far outside His reach. But that's a worry that never comes to pass. Paul goes on: "He has delivered us from such a deadly peril, and he will deliver us. On him we have set our hope that he will continue to deliver us" (2 Cor. 1:10).

Our Shepherd does today for a lost sheep what He did then. It doesn't change. Paul knew it, and we can know it too. "For no matter how many promises God has made, they are 'Yes' in Christ" (2 Cor. 1:20).

The Lord makes His promises and seeks His lost not because of *us* but because of *Him*, because of His love that knows no limits or fear. Because of that great love, we can seek Him and let Him find us, trusting that love to guide us where He needs us to go. Becoming part of His grand plan is our reward, and He grows us for that part a little every day inside the miracles He offers with ease.

> "Though the mountains be shaken and the hills be removed, yet my unfailing love for you will not be shaken nor my covenant of peace be removed," says the LORD.
>
> Isaiah 54:10

We know He'll find us because He promised not to leave us alone or forgotten, and He knows we cannot navigate for ourselves—look how badly things turn out when we're in charge! He prepares to search, and because His love is His divining rod, He finds us just in time, eager and ready for our return. We know He'll search for every lost sheep because He promised, and because we remember He made the pasture.

> The Lord is not slow in keeping his promise, as some understand slowness. He is patient with you, not wanting anyone to perish, but everyone to come to repentance.
>
> 2 Peter 3:9

For Reflection

How has God revealed His promise to find you in whatever "captivity" you're in?

How has His unfailing love shown you how He makes all things possible?

My Shepherd who finds me, thank You for Your faithful promises! Thank You for delivering me from the darkness and choosing my heart for a place to work a miracle. Please help make my promises to You as faithful as Yours are to me. Amen.

Part 5

REDEEMED

For you know that it was not with perishable things such as silver or gold that you were redeemed . . . but with the precious blood of Christ, a lamb without blemish or defect.

1 Peter 1:18–19

Found and loved—that's us! And we hug our Shepherd close, breathing our first breath of peace in such a long time. He has kept true to His promise of a rescue, and another follows—a new beginning for a wayward but wanted sheep. That beginning comes cradled in another promise: His redemption, because being found is only the beginning.

When our Shepherd finds us, He finds us as we are, but He changes us—with His grace. There's no other way to explain it. We can't undo our lostness, but when we are found, we begin a new and deeper walk, where everything in our lives before somehow gets folded into our new skin to become something our Shepherd can groom as He pleases.

And when we surrender to Him and release every fear and doubt we navigated with before, we begin to understand just a little of the love and passion and devotion He has for us. We'll never grasp it all, but that moment when He pulls us to His heart, wraps us in His arms, and says, "You belong to Me," is a great start.

May we cling tightly to Him as we rejoice in our reunion and redemption, as we prepare for the plans He's already made—full and perfect plans especially for you and for me. He's designed a life for each of us where each day is a step toward more light, where our understanding grows and our resolve deepens. We learn much from our time in the dark, but we begin to appreciate it only once we're rescued.

The "treasures of darkness" (Isa. 45:3) come to light when we see what our Shepherd went through to find us and how every step of our travels through the lost and found creates the little sheep He longs to reclaim. No matter how far or how long we stray, our Shepherd hears our calls to return to Him, and He answers. The sooner we call, the sooner our own miracles begin, and the first is that reunion He gets so excited about. We are lifted high and loved, and the best is yet to come.

> Fear not, for I have redeemed you; I have summoned you by name; you are mine.
>
> Isaiah 43:1

For Reflection

How are you prepared to surrender to your Shepherd's lead and accept His grace and redemption?

How will you take your "treasures of darkness" and prepare for the plans He's made for you?

My Shepherd who redeems me, please hold me high and love me through my travels as I learn from the dark and grow in the light. Thank You again for not giving up on me. Amen.

29

REDEEMED . . . AND LOVED

I will be glad and rejoice in your love, for you saw my affliction and
knew the anguish of my soul.

Psalm 31:7

Our anguish comes from being lost, our joy from being found, and
that joy is because of our Shepherd's love. Knowing our wayward
habits and yet accepting us when we ask, He demonstrates His
great love, His reason for searching for us in the first place. And
we can trust His love because it sees us at our worst and remains
faithful anyway.

His love sees what it has to work with and doesn't try to hide. It
sees through all the chaos and mistakes and disappointment to see
even more—the heart of a sheep who wants her Shepherd. And it
says yes—yes to beginning again, to walking with us over a rocky
path to our understanding, to redeeming us with unsurpassed grace.
And that love becomes our hands, enabling us to pass it on. "We
love because he first loved us" (1 John 4:19).

He first *loved* us—not judged us or corrected us or chastised us,
but *loved* us. He established that bond, and because it's stronger

113

than the break we put between Him and ourselves through our wanderings, He uses it to bring us back to Him.

He loves us not because He redeems us. He redeems us because He loves us. He *first* loves us.

Unworthy and still prone to misguidance, we are still so loved by our Shepherd that He will search every pasture to find us, and then He doesn't want to let go. He grabs us that He might give to us the life He knows we need, a life filled with His mercy, grace, guidance, and unending love.

"The LORD is my shepherd, I shall not be in want" (Ps. 23:1). When we understand that we never have to want for His rescue because He always finds us and makes us whole, we can live our lives forever with restored souls and no fear in the pasture of our Shepherd. Being found isn't the end; it's the beginning.

Jesus telegraphed this plan to us long ago when He spoke to Simon about the woman who washed His feet with her tears: "Therefore, I tell you, her many sins have been forgiven—for she loved much" (Luke 7:47). His love lives in our redemption, and our own miracle is about living in our redemption with Him and learning how to pass on His love.

For Reflection

What do you understand about the depth of your Shepherd's love for you?

How much must He love us to redeem us and call us His own?

My Shepherd who redeems me, I am so blessed by
Your great love! Please help me fill my pasture with
Your love and never forget its power or fail to share it
with others. Amen.

30

REDEEMED . . . AND SURE

All who see me mock me; they hurl insults, shaking their heads: "He
trusts in the LORD; let the LORD rescue him. Let him deliver him, since
he delights in him."

Psalm 22:7–8

David's enemies taunted him and dared his Lord to show up when
he called. But David knew the power and devotion and love of
God. He was sure of his Shepherd's faithfulness and unafraid of a
pagan's jabs. We can be the same.

God rescues us from the darkness, and we can trust Him in the
light. He doesn't do it for the thrill of bringing us back from a misguided trip; He will remain with us, guide us every step we allow,
and yes, even find us again when we go astray.

We can put away the doubts about His love and pursuit because
we've experienced it firsthand, deep down to our darkness. We know
He answers when a lost sheep cries because that has happened to
us many times over.

And no matter how others ridicule us or question our faith, we can respond with complete confidence. How much more proof does anyone need than someone who's been there? And that's you and me—little sheep so loved by their Shepherd that He finds us and makes us whole again.

> Let us draw near to God with a sincere heart in full assurance of faith. . . . Let us hold unswervingly to the hope we profess, for he who promised is faithful.
>
> Hebrews 10:22–23

Our redemption means our renewal, our return to the Shepherd who has the power and will to unveil for us the life He's planned. With every comforting squeeze, we get a peek at who we can become because of the effort He's making. We definitely know what a disaster we are when left to our own control, and we discover a little more each day about how full our future is when left to God's leadership.

We can face those who might doubt our Shepherd and even face our own fears of repeated lostness when we remember the reunion and everything that comes with it—a new beginning wrapped in His grace and a part of His plan for which He'll prepare us.

The pasture of His redemption is fertile indeed.

For Reflection

How do you respond to doubters?

How sure are you of your Shepherd's love and redemption, now and forever?

My Shepherd who redeems me, please make me quick
to put to rest anyone's questions about Your love and
loyalty. Help me trust Your faithful response and
match my own to it. Amen.

31

REDEEMED . . . AND READY

Into your hands I commit my spirit; redeem me, O LORD, the God of truth.

Psalm 31:5

We're overjoyed when we're found and bow our heads at God's knee to express our gratitude. And in that place of reunion, we discover something else—we're ready to move on, to go forward, released from the darkness into an infinite light that beckons us to follow. We're ready for the joys and blessings and victories our Shepherd has planned for us.

When our Shepherd looks at our grateful hearts, He also looks for our willing hearts, for our surrender to Him to lead the way. Do we meet Him by committing our spirits? Are we ready to give ourselves over to Him so that the reunion begets the beginning *He* wants?

Our belief in His faithfulness and our readiness to submit to Him allows Him to take all we are and show us all we can become for

Him here on earth. There's little more that He asks for. We can see the perfect example in the young David.

The shepherd boy matched his trust in the Lord (he was sure) with his skills (he was ready) to score the most stunning underdog victory of all time. When we're faced with seemingly overwhelming odds, we too can respond as David did: "You come against me with sword and spear and javelin, but I come against you in the name of the LORD Almighty" (1 Sam. 17:45).

When our focus is on the Lord who rescued us, and we offer ourselves completely—even if we feel we have little to give—the result will be victory for us too.

The Goliaths in our lives will come disguised as many things, and they'll seem big and all-powerful. Maybe they'll come from within as jealousy or anger, or from without as betrayal or denial, but the call to arms is the same. God will help us fight these battles when we're ready—and willing—to give Him access to everything we are and then draw back in complete faith in His strength. And His redemption—the truth through which we are found and made whole—makes it all possible.

In the light, our eyes are opened to all He's prepared us with, to our past and present that propel us to accomplish His will. We can look within ourselves and see all we've learned, unlearned, and relearned to make us ready to face foes big and small.

We can trust that we're ready when God puts us there, toe to toe in the trenches, and demands we make a choice—run away or work with what we have. And when we put what we have in His hands, there is never any reason to run.

We can also trust that when we need to be *made* ready for something new, He can handle that little detail. And our willing hearts just keep growing.

For Reflection

How has God prepared you for this time in your life?

What makes you willing and able to respond to the Goliaths you face?

> *My Shepherd who redeems me, please make me ready like David, unafraid and sure of victory over the dangers in my life. Please help me commit my spirit with enthusiasm and confidence. Amen.*

32

REDEEMED . . . AND WISE

If any of you lacks wisdom, he should ask God, who gives generously to all without finding fault, and it will be given to him. But when he asks, he must believe and not doubt.

James 1:5–6

We certainly need some wisdom, don't we? We need to know how to stay on our path, how to avoid the darkness. And we needn't worry. We can have that wisdom because God grants it in His grace. He deals with us on a need-to-know basis, and that's all we need to know.

Our pasture is never a place we walk alone. Our Shepherd is here. And we don't need a slide rule or a dictionary to understand His redemption or our next step. We need to remember only that He will faithfully *find* us, and then we can trust that He will faithfully *teach* us what we need to know. He always makes us wise enough for the next step because "those who are wayward in spirit will gain understanding" (Isa. 29:24).

Being found puts us in the classroom in which we learn best—one where our minds and hearts are open and trusting. Our Shepherd's grace reaches down to our misunderstanding of His unmatched love and desire for us and shows us another piece of the puzzle, a part we will play with unique aptitude.

When He redeems us—He answers our plea for forgiveness and rescue—He buys us back from the lostness that swallowed us. He trades our ignorance and rebellion for His mercy and guidance. We benefit from an abundance of riches that are ours for the taking if we choose, including great wisdom for the many choices to come.

When we make ourselves ready to work and ready to learn, we're then ready to discover all the wisdom God's chosen to entrust to us. He won't ask us to do anything we can't because He's the giver of the ability. See how well it works? Our job is to follow where He leads and trust the route and reasons to Him.

Wisdom Delivered

"I am sending you out like sheep among wolves. Therefore be as shrewd as snakes and as innocent as doves," Jesus tells us (Matt. 10:16). And how do we do that except through the wisdom He gives us? It follows that we can ask for direction and understanding and perspective when we need them, and they will be revealed to us. And we don't ever have to worry if Jesus will respond on time. In captivity to darkness of any kind, we can trust our Shepherd to know what and when we need to know and to make sure that we do too.

> Do not worry about what to say or how to say it. At that time you will be given what to say, for it will not be you speaking, but the Spirit of your Father speaking through you.
>
> Matthew 10:19–20

We're redeemed because He rescues and we repent. We're made wise because He teaches and we learn. The next move is ours to respond.

For Reflection

How do you feel when God is teaching you and helping you discover your wisdom?

What are some experiences from your life where His wisdom guided you in difficult choices?

My Shepherd who redeems me, please grant me the blessings of Your wisdom so that I will know how to follow You and play my part in Your great plan. Please teach me everything I need to know. Amen.

33

REDEEMED ... AND RESPONSIVE

Surely you have granted him eternal blessings and made him glad
with the joy of your presence.

Psalm 21:6

We read about the Israelites rebuilding the wall of Jerusalem in the
book of Nehemiah. It was after a long time of lostness and division
that Nehemiah rallied the troops, and they came together under
threats to their lives and difficult working conditions to restore the
wall in a few weeks.

After the wall was completed, Nehemiah called everyone together
to hear the reading of God's words. For seven or eight days, the
people heard about God's faithfulness and were reminded of the
lack of their own. They had failed God, but He had found them
and loved them and restored them. The enormity and generosity
of His grace in response to their misguidance made them upset and
ashamed. They cried. But Nehemiah urged a different response:

> This day is sacred to the LORD your God. Do not mourn or weep. . . .
> Go and enjoy choice food and sweet drinks, and send some to those
> who have nothing prepared. This day is sacred to our LORD. Do not
> grieve, for the joy of the LORD is your strength.
>
> Nehemiah 8:9–10

And they did. They celebrated "with great joy, because they now understood the words that had been made known to them" (v. 12). They even reinstated the Feast of Booths, a celebration to remind the Israelites of their rescue from Egypt and deliverance to the Promised Land. Now home themselves, the people responded to God's redemption. "The whole company that had returned from exile built booths and lived in them. From the days of Joshua son of Nun until that day, the Israelites had not celebrated it like this. And their joy was very great" (v. 17).

God waits for us to respond to His grace and redemption the same way—with celebration and generosity and action and joy. The building of the wall was an outward sign of the condition of the people's hearts. They belonged to their Shepherd and He delighted in their company. He made them willing and able to be a part of His plan, and they responded.

We may have our own walls to build, or even to tear down, and it may take a few weeks or a few years, but one thing we can know for sure: our Shepherd is waiting for our response to our rescue. He says to weep no more; the best is yet to be. The more we know and understand, the more He expects and makes possible.

The rainbow in the rescue reflects our response. God makes it as bright as we want.

For Reflection

How do you respond to God's redemption—with weeping or rejoicing?

What kind of walls are waiting for you to build or tear down?

My Shepherd who redeems me, please stay with me
and help me respond with joy to meet Your will.
Help me remember You're focused on the future
and I should be too, because Your plan awaits.
Amen.

34

Redeemed . . .
and Accountable

Do your best to present yourself to God as one approved, a work-
man who does not need to be ashamed and who correctly handles
the word of truth.

2 Timothy 2:15

God never wastes anything, and He doesn't expect us to either.
The great wisdom and abilities we gain through our redemption
do more than demonstrate our Shepherd's mercy and love. They
become a part of us, a guiding light we must not ignore.

Everything we gain when our Shepherd finds us serves to protect
us from the dangers of lostness all around. It's our joy and delight
to follow this new path we've been given. But the new road comes
with responsibility.

We're expected to use everything we know everywhere we go.
God allows us to work in places of decisions and challenges so that
we may trust Him to guide us and show Him what we've learned.

We will not be expected to do more than we're capable of, but we will also not be expected to do less.

Nothing we gain in our rescue is fluff or window dressing. We experience and learn and understand so that we can put all we know into practice, and then we experience and learn and understand some more. And if we squander or neglect our lessons, the consequences are painful.

The priest Ezekiel tells God's story of the watchman in Ezekiel 33:1–6. If someone ignores the warnings of danger a watchman sounds, that's his own fault. But if the watchman fails to warn the people and someone dies, God says, "I will hold the watchman accountable for his blood" (v. 6). Likewise, we have a responsibility to relay what we know, and we do it best in the lives we lead.

> Guard the good deposit that was entrusted to you—guard it with the help of the Holy Spirit who lives in us.
>
> 2 Timothy 1:14

We don't enjoy our redemption in a vacuum or at a finish line—we are always at risk of the dangers of this world, and others are too. The darkness always looms right ahead, yet when we've been blessed with forgiveness of our mistakes and an understanding of how to better follow our Shepherd, we are more able to make good choices for ourselves that all can see.

By living lives influenced by God, we can stand before Him, eager to answer for the paths we've taken. May He never hold us accountable for leading another sheep astray by the daily actions of our lives. "Do not cause anyone to stumble" (1 Cor. 10:32).

We probably won't serve as watchmen for entire cities, but God still arranges for us to serve in what we know. Whoever sees you may think, "She's a loyal sheep of the Shepherd," or perhaps something less flattering based on what he or she witnesses. Every day and every relationship is a chance to sound the alarm. That choice is His gift and our responsibility. Sometimes we get it right. Sometimes we have more to learn.

For Reflection

Have you ever been the lazy watchman with your actions? If so, what happened?

How does your life reflect your rescue, and are you comfortable answering to God for your choices?

What would you like to change?

> *My Shepherd who redeems me, please make me eager*
> *and able to use all the grace and abilities You've given*
> *me in everything I do. Please help me waste nothing.*
> *Amen.*

35

REDEEMED ... AND IMPERFECT

Who is a God like you, who pardons sin and forgives the transgression of the remnant of his inheritance? You do not stay angry forever but delight to show mercy. You will again have compassion on us; you will tread our sins underfoot and hurl all our iniquities into the depths of the sea.

Micah 7:18–19

Our God who knows all knows us so well. He knows our flaws, and no matter how many we correct and how wise we become, we will never be free of our imperfections in this world. We'll always have our human tendency to get lost, but that doesn't mean our Shepherd gives up on us. We've learned He works with what He has, including us, so that His way prevails. We are forever the student sheep of the powerful Shepherd.

When David learned of God's promises through Nathan the prophet—that He would love him forever (see 2 Sam. 7:15) and make his kingdom endure forever (see v. 16)—he was amazed at God's generosity and commitment: "Who am I, O Sovereign

LORD, and what is my family, that you have brought me this far?" (v. 18).

As David learned, despite his many missteps and times spent wandering in the dark, his Shepherd always answered his humble call. When David offered himself to God—again and again—God responded because David's genuine humility and continued willingness to learn meant more than his human imperfections. May we know the same rescue again and again.

David knew that God understood how far from perfect he was: "What more can David say to you? For you know your servant, O Sovereign LORD" (v. 20). God knew that David, even especially chosen and blessed beyond compare, was still like all of us—a loved sheep who would stray from time to time. But still He promised His grace and guidance. And David responded with surrender to God's plan:

> O LORD Almighty, God of Israel, you have revealed this to your servant, saying, "I will build a house for you." So your servant has found courage to offer you this prayer. O Sovereign LORD, you are God! Your words are trustworthy, and you have promised these good things to your servant. Now be pleased to bless the house of your servant, that it may continue forever in your sight.
>
> verses 27–29

David was saying, "Not because of my perfection but because of Yours, my Shepherd, may Your will be done." Imperfect but unafraid, David offered himself to God, knowing he would have much to learn, yet blessed with a Shepherd devoted and patient enough to teach him.

> I am the true vine, and my Father is the gardener. . . . Remain in me, and I will remain in you. No branch can bear fruit by itself; it must remain in the vine. . . . I am the vine; you are the branches. If a man remains in me and I in him, he will bear much fruit; apart from me you can do nothing.
>
> John 15:1, 4–5

David's job was to learn and obey and grow into the branch God picked him to be. Our task isn't so different today. Our imperfections won't disappear, but the more we remain in our Shepherd, the more opportunity He has to work around those flaws. We either bear fruit despite our imperfections or wither away in them. God's grace makes it possible to choose fruit.

I Want to Be a Potato

When I was a kid, I wasn't crazy about much of the work in our vegetable garden, but I loved digging potatoes. Of course, my dad did the actual digging when the vines died and the signs were right. To be sure it was time, he'd gently turn over a shovelful of dirt under a few plants to check the hidden crop. I'd wait for him to say, "Yep, today's the day." He'd go down the rows, unearthing piles of soil to release the treasure. Then it was my turn.

I'd dig my hands into the clumpy soil, searching for the potato bounty. Sometimes I'd find small ones, but that was okay. They were best unpeeled and cooked atop green beans. Sometimes I'd find great big ones and know how good they'd taste fried in my mom's iron skillet. It took hours to get them all. I'd brush away the clingy Alabama dirt and pile them in little piles along the rows. Then we'd carry them in buckets or a wheelbarrow to their special place—the dark, dry wooden floor of the shed with the shallow lime blanket already prepared.

My dad would spread all the potatoes out—except for the ones my mom would ferry inside for the week's suppers—and then cover them with just a little more lime. And the potatoes were perfect just like that.

And much to my joy, there was no shucking or silking or shelling or cutting or canning to follow! I wish I could be a potato for God—needing so little to do so much, low-maintenance, and nearly perfect.

But no, I'm more like that impatient corn that *has* to be pulled when it's ready and then shucked and silked and washed and cut and cooked before it can be perfect. And sometimes I'm like the prickly okra that fights back or the sneaky cucumber that makes me hunt under the vines and still gets away.

I'm so glad the Master Gardener likes corn and okra and cucumbers, so glad He doesn't shy away from all the work like a kid who'd rather do *anything* than shell another bushel of peas. He knows I'm a lot of work, but it doesn't matter to Him. The end result is all He sees, and the journey is a time for new growth—a time to help me recover what I've lost, mend what's broken, and work where no one can see to become the fruit He needs me to be.

In the soil of my heart, my Shepherd takes everything I am and makes it perfect for what He needs, one season at a time. Maybe one day I'll be a potato, but every day I'll be loved and redeemed by my Shepherd, a needy little sheep ready to grow.

For Reflection

How do you call to God when your imperfections have led you astray again?

Why does He answer and how do you respond?

> *My Shepherd who redeems me, please always see past my flaws and love me and redeem me with Your infinite grace. Help me grow into the branch You've chosen me to be so that Your will is done. Amen.*

Part 6

GROWING

For the eyes of the Lord are on the righteous and his ears are attentive to their prayer.

1 Peter 3:12

Found and redeemed, we're now able to grow, to change, to become all we're capable of becoming because our Shepherd has called us by name. He scoops us up and shapes us the way He wants because He has a plan.

Our part begins and ends with prayer, because in that intimate communication with Him, we see what He sees. Never by our own power but always buoyed by His grace we grow. And then we grow some more. It's a bumper crop of blessings.

Like a tender tomato vine, we're pliable in our Shepherd's hands when we're experiencing the glow of a life redeemed by His grace. We're so grateful and sometimes still in awe—at least, I am—of His desperate care for a sheep with such a poor sense of direction. And we find ourselves in a state of pure worship.

We've learned that He has a pasture for us and paths in it for a reason. When we let Him lead, our little grass-munching lives are so much more peaceful—not uneventful or untouched by this world, but *peaceful* because we know we rest in Him. And following His lead means growing in understanding, trust, and obedience to Him. He knows well our stubborn ways, but He also knows how to use every circumstance and experience to get us where we need to be.

Growing is a life choice we make every day, and knowing our forgetful natures, the Shepherd has given us a guided prayer to help us. Prayer is the first step in our growing walk with Him. It's our connection to our Guide, a constant string of signs for our travels that He unveils as we interact with Him. Our Shepherd grows us for His pleasure and will, and our lives change when we choose to follow Him. This is how we pray and grow.

For Reflection

How eager are you to grow toward your Shepherd as a plant reaches for the light?

How do you pray to hear God's guidance?

My Shepherd who grows me, what a green thumb You must have! Please work Your miracles in my life as You grow me into all You know I can be. Amen.

36

GROWING WITH PRAYER

He answered their prayers, because they trusted in him.

1 Chronicles 5:20

Sometimes we have a love/hate relationship with our prayers. If we get a yes, we're happy and say a thank-you prayer. If we get a no, we complain, question God, or pout and move on to another request. If we don't get an answer at all and have to wait, we get impatient and fussy. We're used to a world of point-and-click responses where a few extra seconds are unpardonable.

I'm not sure our Shepherd meant for His precious sheep to keep such a narrow focus on the great communication system He provided. When we make our prayers fit a "go/no go" gauge, we miss out on their beauty and power. We pray *for* things and always will because we're needy little sheep. That's a communication we understand well, and that's okay.

But our Shepherd craves the prayers that change us as we pray *through* things, our prayers that become a silent testimony of how

He's growing all the purposes He's planted in our hearts. Those prayers are truly a wonderful exchange that never ends.

Crying Prayer

> In my anguish I cried to the LORD, and he answered by setting me free.
>
> Psalm 118:5

Some of our most remembered prayers are prayers of desperation— when we've given up finding a way out of whatever mess we're in, and we just sit down alone and cry for our Shepherd. And His answer is always the same, because He won't turn away from our pain.

His answer is always to rescue us from our lostness, to set us free by bringing us in. In His pasture, we're free from the anguish and fears and isolation of a deep darkness. We're free to kick and scream within His pasture and approach Him with all our questions and doubts. We're free to live without fear because we know He watches the gates and fences and will protect our hearts with His power. We're free to face Him and cry some more.

We're free to go to our Shepherd and pray about anything. There is no banned subject where prayer is concerned. And we need not be worried about His reaction or embarrassed by our lack of know-how. No one sees our prayer but our Shepherd, who's already seen us at our worst. Prayer is a private dance between God and us. "When you pray, go into your room, close the door and pray to your Father" (Matt. 6:6).

That knowledge both comforts and challenges me: *I have God's full attention!* I am free to plead my case, ask for forgiveness, and cry for His mercy and guidance. And that's as it should be. No matter what's happening with the other ninety-nine sheep, I am reminded that what's happening with me matters too. I breathe a prayer and He is here.

A long or wordy prayer doesn't mean a better prayer. "When you pray, do not keep on babbling like pagans, for they think they will be heard because of their many words" (Matt. 6:7). Only one word truly matters.

When It's Hard

We know that prayer is not a mindless activity. But what about the times you feel you don't have the power to think it through, when you feel you can't pray? You *can*, I promise. Your prayer may be only *God* or *Father* or *Please* or *Help*. The structure of your thoughts isn't important, but your growth with each breath is.

That's because any time you pray, you're growing in obedience and surrender to God—because you're asking with expectation, trusting that your Shepherd is still looking for you, still able to guide you, still able to free you from the darkness. That's praying on your travels through the lost and found.

Sometimes I think those prayers are the most pure and effective—when we don't petition God or bargain with Him or discuss or argue. Instead we simply surrender. We stop trying to navigate our way, and we call upon the One whose trust we should have depended on long ago. I think those prayers put us most in line with His will, when in our desperation to grow and understand, we finally realize and believe that our Father knows what we need before we ask Him (see Matt. 6:8).

The Word That Matters

While all prayer is wonderful and essential to our understanding of our Shepherd's ways, the prayers that begin and end with His name make the greatest starting place. These prayers put us where we need to be.

We decide how tall and strong we grow in knowing and following our Shepherd according to how we pray. We grow best when we pray continually, in surrender, because only when we keep our hearts focused on Him and our trust in His wisdom can we explore the vast reaches of the pasture He made for us. We can know these wonders only through our prayers. And He shows us how to enjoy and grow in this beautiful intimacy with Him every moment.

> Our Father in heaven,
> hallowed be your name,
> your kingdom come,
> your will be done
>> on earth as it is in heaven.
> Give us today our daily bread.
> Forgive us our debts,
>> as we also have forgiven our debtors.
> And lead us not into temptation,
> but deliver us from the evil one.
>
> Matthew 6:9–13

For Reflection

How do you pray, and what do you do with God's response?

How do you pray when praying is hard?

> *My Shepherd who grows me, please help me*
> *understand our prayer connection and always trust*
> *that Your answers to all my prayers are the best.*
> *Please grow me with my every word. Amen.*

37

GROWING TRUST OF
WHO GOD IS

Our Father in heaven, hallowed be your name.
Matthew 6:9

The prayer that matters most, the prayer of *Father*, really says it all.
We're revering Him and praising Him and recognizing Him as our
Shepherd, knowing that He hears us because He promised and He's
close by, inside our hearts even.

The pursuit in tandem with Him that got us here and the plea
to stay within our perfect pasture lead us to a daily decision—will
we trust God *still* to be who He says He is after we are found? Will
we trust Him to shepherd us wisely and know our needs and be
all He promised? Will we trust Him to be "our Father" today when
we cry and tomorrow when we don't? Will we trust Him to know
what's in our hearts when *Father* is all we can pray?

Growing up means growing sure of who He is.

For us there is but one God, the Father, from whom all things came and for whom we live; and there is but one Lord, Jesus Christ, through whom all things came and through whom we live.

1 Corinthians 8:6

A Burning Choice

Ahab ruled over Israel for twenty-two years, and during that time, he "did more evil in the eyes of the LORD than any of those before him" (1 Kings 16:30). We read about how he built a temple to Baal, the Canaanite god of fertility, and promoted his worship among all the people. Meanwhile, Elijah, Israel's prophet, relayed God's message that there would be a drought in the land (see 17:1), and that's exactly what happened.

Elijah, though, was rescued from hunger and thirst, while the Israelites endured the dry and barren land—so representative of their lack of commitment to their Father. Finally, Elijah told them to make a choice whether or not to trust God to be who He says He is and to obey Him. Grow in your faith, he said, or die (spiritually) without it. "If the LORD is God, follow him; but if Baal is God, follow him" (18:21). It's a choice we make every day.

But the people didn't jump behind Elijah and march in step to follow their Lord all of a sudden. They wanted something more, so Elijah arranged for a dramatic display of God's power. He and the prophets of Baal prepared sacrifices as the people waited in suspense.

Those noisy prophets of Baal danced and shouted for their god for hours, but no fire consumed their sacrifices. I love Elijah's response. Perhaps it's a little cocky, but it's bathed in pure faith and confidence in his Father:

At noon Elijah began to taunt them. "Shout louder!" he said. "Surely he is a god! Perhaps he is deep in thought, or busy, or traveling. Maybe he is sleeping and must be awakened."

1 Kings 18:27

All day the prophets called to a false and useless god who never answered. Then Elijah made the wager even more interesting. He soaked his wood and offering three times with four large jars of water. Then he *prayed*:

> O LORD, God of Abraham, Isaac and Israel, let it be known today that you are God in Israel and that I am your servant and have done all these things at your command. Answer me, O LORD, answer me, so these people will know that you, O LORD, are God, and that you are turning their hearts back again.
>
> 1 Kings 18:36–37

The results were amazing but not unpredictable to God's obedient servant, as "the fire of the LORD fell and burned up the sacrifice, the wood, the stones and the soil, and also licked up the water in the trench" (v. 38).

And then the people were found again and no doubt eager to learn and grow in their walk with the all-powerful and only God who is everything He says, who is Father to us all.

An Everyday Choice

Our obedience dilemma today may not be choosing between a foreign god and our own, but it may be choosing anything that threatens to diminish our Shepherd in our eyes so that we're led astray and trapped in the darkness.

So in faith and obedience, we pray every day, *Our Father in heaven, hallowed be Thy name. Help me remember who You are, and give me the trust of Elijah and the assurance of Your presence. Guide me away from any "foreign god" that would endanger our relationship, because I know You alone are my Father, and every day that I'm closer to You, my faith grows even more. Remind me that praying* Father *is enough.*

As we grow more and more into the disciples God has planned us to be, the dangers like those from Baal or the twenty-first century become less and less impressive. We follow God not out of fear or obligation but out of joy and reverence. It's a choice—and it's one our treacherous, trap-filled world forces on us. Fortunately, like a well-trained soldier, we are prepared by our Shepherd.

> Make plans by seeking advice; if you wage war, obtain guidance.
>
> Proverbs 20:18

Okay! We're ready to grow the way God has planned, but what do we do? Do we strike off in the first direction we see? Uh . . . better not—that's often what gets us lost. Maybe we should think a while, consult someone smarter than we are.

It's no accident that the prayer Jesus modeled for us begins with "Our Father." Those words alone put us in His presence and put our pliable hearts and souls in His hands. Real growth must begin from our roots grounded in who our Shepherd is—because that trust and faith is what makes every other part of the prayer make sense. Without that beginning, nothing follows.

So we learn to wage war against all the misguidance and the lostness and the aloneness and the fear of not being found by calling on our Father for help—by growing so close to Him that our first unconscious move is to bend toward His heart, to listen for His directions. He promises His guidance to us over and over, and growing up means growing sure that He will not withhold it, because He is our Shepherd who leads every one of His sheep, even us stubborn ones bent on taking the wrong path sometimes.

Choosing Trust

As we depend on our trust in Him and call upon it to guide us in His will, we grow into the mature sheep He knows we can be. And we avoid so many missteps we made in the past, not because we've grown perfect but because we've grown more secure in our trust, more willing to bank on that unexplainable love our Shepherd has for us. He's given us so much, and we finally can give Him something back—a will of our own to do His.

We grow into more when we start from that humble place we know He understands, when our prayer of *Father* is enough. He wraps us in His arms and says, *I'm your Father and I'm here. You never have to be afraid again.* And we believe Him.

For Reflection

How can you show the confidence of Elijah when false gods try to sway you?

How do you feel when you can pray only *Father*?

Can you trust that *Father* is enough, and then feel Him close and hear Him respond?

My Shepherd who grows me, thank You for understanding when I can barely pray at all. Thank You for being everything by being You and never going away. Amen.

38

GROWING TRUST IN HIS CONTROL

Your kingdom come, your will be done on earth as it is in heaven.

Matthew 6:10

This part of the prayer can be one of the toughest parts for us "I know better" sheep. We might like to change those words to "C'mon, Lord, do *my* will, here and everywhere." That would just about cover it, and we'd be fine and dandy, wouldn't we? But I've yet to see that petition recommended anywhere in His Word. Have you?

Perhaps this approach isn't best because sheep aren't known for their great powers of discernment and long-range planning. But what are we to do? We have to live in the pasture, where we're responsible for choosing our way every day. We have to follow the will of something, and it's completely our choice.

Teach me to do your will, for you are my God; may your good Spirit lead me on level ground.

Psalm 143:10

Learning and living this part of the prayer means growing in our trust that God's in control of everything that happens. This choice comes in two parts: praying to work within the will of God (part 1) and offering ourselves to become a part of His will on earth (part 2).

Part 1

Scraggly, disoriented sheep that I am, I don't pretend to understand the Lord's all-encompassing will. Who can foretell the future of our world? But that big question doesn't have to be my focus. I know my mind can't wrap itself around something so massive. But I can focus on His will within *my* life. I can work there.

When we can truly leave the global landscape to our Shepherd and trust Him to alter it as He sees fit, we can walk on the plot of "level ground" before us. We can trust that He's in control even when we can't see the ground, which is a lot of the time in most of our messy, complicated lives. When we follow Him and trust in Him because He told us to, we can also believe that He knows what's going on and feel secure—because He told us to.

That trust is one of the choices we make as we grow in obedience to the Lord. I can't force you to make that choice, but I can promise He will never make you regret it if you do. Your trust in His control will never be betrayed or taken for granted or abused. We can make that choice safely because He told us to. And as we obey one choice at a time, we carry on.

Part 2

One day we'll get to heaven and see God's wise and guiding hand in everything, from *His* perspective, where it all fits. Right now, though, we can see only the parts that touch us in our lives here on earth, and thanks to Him, that's where we get to play our parts. Because we're perfectly suited to the atmosphere, I guess we're a good fit. There must be someone wise in control, wouldn't you agree?

As we trust in God's will and believe He knows best, we still have to do something besides stand in our pasture all day. We were made to move, to work, to share, to encourage, to teach—*to do God's will.* "In him we were also chosen, having been predestined according to the plan of him who works out everything in conformity with the purpose of his will" (Eph. 1:11). He has everything planned. Will we be a part?

We pray for that priceless experience. We ask our Shepherd to show us how to be a part of His will here on earth, in our pasture. Sure, He can accomplish His pleasure without our help, but we are the ones who miss out on an incredible life when we don't ask to be a part of His plan.

When we've handed our lives over to Him, trusting in His control when we do understand and when we don't, we're free to move on to the parts we can always play and understand on earth—the living, breathing actions we take in our small but not insignificant way to help make His will alive.

Our prayer becomes *Lord, please make me a part of Your will here. Please teach me and grow me into a map for others, a safe passage, and a branch in bloom.*

Plenty of Options

Chances abound for us to become a part of His plan. We might become a signpost for someone else and keep her from getting lost. We might provide comfort for those lost and help them out of the darkness. We might help others grow while we do, stretching our faith to meet theirs. We might be an example that proves to others exactly how in control our Shepherd really is. We too can live our lives in the way that says, "I have come to do your will, O God" (Heb. 10:7).

By using the trust we're growing in every day, we find level ground here in our pasture, no matter what the ground is like beyond the borders of our hearts. It's a foundation that builds with practice and belief. And we have plenty of opportunities because God is never short of parts for us to play—maybe big parts like careers, maybe small parts like kindness.

Ask Him and believe what He tells you. Trust in His control and your ability to hear Him. He will never lead you astray but will lead you on level ground to a perfect destination He has chosen, "for it is God who works in you to will and to act according to his good purpose" (Phil. 2:13).

Seeing Clearly

Sometimes our view is clouded by our own disheveled fur and our interpretation of what we think best. Sometimes we just don't see what God sees because our focus is too rigid, too immature to allow for something bigger, and too afraid to trust. But we don't have to be afraid, and this calm and security comes from a wisdom that grows with our trust. Jesus pointed out just how narrow-minded we can be when He urged the Jews to grow in their judgment:

> Jesus said to them, "I did one miracle, and you are all astonished. Yet because Moses gave you circumcision . . . you circumcise a child on the Sabbath. Now if a child can be circumcised on the Sabbath so that the law of Moses may not be broken, why are you angry with me for healing the whole man on the Sabbath? Stop judging by mere appearances, and make a right judgment."
>
> John 7:21–24

When we trust in God's control of our moments and the whole world forever, we judge more rightly too, because we have something to guide us—a belief that He knows what He's doing, on earth as in heaven. The limits we try to place on an unlimited God only keep us from growing closer to Him, from being part of the plans

He's made for our benefit. In obedience, though, we can genuinely and sincerely pray for His will, knowing that doing so broadens our understanding and rewards our trust—and that result is His will also.

The more control we relinquish to Him, the less lost we'll become. Our energies go into growing and becoming what He's already planned.

> Do not conform any longer to the pattern of this world, but be transformed by the renewing of your mind. Then you will be able to test and approve what God's will is—his good, pleasing and perfect will.
>
> Romans 12:2

For Reflection

How do you sometimes want to supplant your will in place of God's?

How will a deepening trust in His control affect your efforts to do His will on earth?

My Shepherd who grows me, in Your control I can rest. Your will must be best because You would never get me lost. Please help me trust Your plan and be a part of it. Amen.

39

GROWING TRUST IN HIS PRESENCE

Give us today our daily bread.

Matthew 6:11

Because of the "everything's a crisis" life that most of us head-strong sheep live, we have ample opportunity to learn this part of the prayer. No matter how much we plan and arrange and try to control everything, sooner or later, we learn that this moment, this day, are all we have, and we are in control of nothing.

I imagine God wonders why it takes us so long and so many walks in the darkness to figure this one out, but there we are, fussy and obstinate and not wanting to admit how helpless we are. Perhaps He mostly wonders why we misunderstand and deprive ourselves of His precious and complete "daily bread" by looking past it, why this moment, this day, never seems to be enough for us.

So do we give up making plans for our future? Of course not, but trusting that future to our Shepherd begins with trusting this moment, this day. And He'll use any situation to make that clear to us. In the darkest of times, He'll shine so much light that our trust in His presence will grow like the cedars of Lebanon—strong and true, always yielding what He wishes.

One Day at a Time

Eight days before Christmas, my husband had an accident. I arrived at the emergency room to find him awaiting X-rays, his new jeans ripped from hem to zipper to accommodate the doctor's probing hands. He thought he'd get some crutches and then we'd go home.

A few hours later, I sat in the dimly lit surgery waiting room. My husband had broken both legs.

One leg was broken worse than the other and pushed backward at the knee. He needed a plate and screws for it. The surgeon said he wouldn't stand for at least six weeks and couldn't work for maybe six months. When I went to him in the recovery room, I'd never seen anyone in so much pain. He'd never even been a patient in the hospital before, and there he was, immobile and drugged, with the medication doing little to help. Four days later, he went home on a stretcher, with splints and thirty-eight stitches flanking his left knee.

I wanted so much to hurt for him, but all I could do was cry for both of us. People kept asking me questions, and I didn't have any answers. This wasn't a stomachache or the flu; the whole thing was brand-new—horribly, numbingly new. I didn't know anything except when it was time for medication and where extra pillows were to elevate his legs. Our lives revolved around pain and fear and the terrifying sense of not knowing. Life as we had known it stopped. Christmas came and went.

We brought in a hospital bed for my husband, complete with trapeze bar, but even then he could barely move. I slept on the couch next to him, three or four hours a night if we were lucky. Then we'd face another day of what we quickly accepted—pain for him and trying to help for me.

We were both exhausted. I lived in chopped-up sections of time, trying to make him something to eat while his sheets were washed, dress his incision while they dried, and change his bed while he tried to move and couldn't. Day and night were all the same, because everything was about facing something neither of us knew anything about, wondering what would happen next and almost afraid to ask out loud.

But inside my head during this time was one of those running prayers that never seem to begin or end. It was just there, all the time. Perhaps my prayer was out of fear and panic at first, but soon it was out of awe and gratitude and complete faith. That may seem like an unusual twist, but in my most fearful darkness, I came to know my greatest peace.

My faith grew one day at a time because I could think through only one day at a time. I could only see through the pain *today*, only talk to God about what challenges we had to meet *today*. There was little thought of after today, when things returned to normal—if they ever would. There was always only this moment, this day, when my Shepherd would provide the strength and guidance for my next step. It's not a bad plan for any day.

Throughout my husband's recovery, the conversation in my head never stopped. There was my pleading, my questions, my pain, my surrender—all matched by my Shepherd's comfort, reassurance, grace, peace for that moment, that day.

My daily bread of His presence never left me hungry. He met me lost and empty, then rescued me and filled me morning to night with the nourishment I needed—His control of *me*.

When I thought surely I was going to break and crumble, He cultivated in me more trust than I'd ever known, one day at a time. When that trust was all I could see, all I could grasp, it turned out that it was right—perfect even—because trust grows best when it has the whole garden to itself.

For Reflection

When have you had a hard time focusing on just today?

What happens when you can rely on nothing but God's presence?

> *My Shepherd who grows me, thank You for giving me only one day at a time to live. Please help me grow my trust that You will show up every day and grant me everything I need. Amen.*

40

GROWING TRUST IN HIS PLAN

Forgive us our debts, as we also have forgiven our debtors.

Matthew 6:12

Trust in God's plan means doing our part in it, wherever we find to do it. And so we pray, *Make me like You, Lord; trust me with part of Your plan.*

He says, *Okay, but know My plan is always forward.*

Yeah, I got that, not looking back into the darkness and all. The divine plan is for us to pass on what we've been given, to be a breathing example of incredible trust in our Shepherd, and to follow Him and His ways.

In Prayerful Peace

The only way we can forgive as He teaches, for example, is to trust that His plan for whatever happens to us can be reached only if we surrender our lives to Him. It takes great obedience to forgive and to follow His other leads, but we can do it when our reason is borne out of our trust in His plan, His wisdom, and His strength.

So we obey and forgive, and when we make that a habit, peace finds us no matter what else is happening around us. Peter knew that even in prison, because he knew how to use what his Shepherd had taught him:

> The night before Herod was to bring him to trial, Peter was sleeping between two soldiers, bound with two chains, and sentries stood guard at the entrance.
>
> Acts 12:6

Did you see that? Peter was *sleeping*! Bound and imprisoned, he was at peace because he trusted in his Father's plan. And he passed it on by the way he lived his life.

We learn deep trust and other skills because they somehow play a part in *our* part of God's plan, even though it may be hard to understand sometimes. We always learn the most trust at the hardest times, through the most difficult situations. Then we see that every opportunity to forgive, help, minister, lead, or demonstrate our peace and security is part of the whole.

Miraculous things happen when we forgive, love, and teach as God has forgiven, loved, and taught us. His plan makes us *more* because we listen and obey, because we trust and follow. Everything we touch in trust touches someone else.

As we grow our trust in His plan, we too can do whatever is required of us. We can be like Peter. When we stay in prayer, we stay in His presence, and trusting becomes like breathing. It truly keeps us going when we think we can't go on.

The Plan Continues

The Israelites were lost in the desert for forty years because they disobeyed God. But because He is the Shepherd who seeks His sheep and still has a plan, He gave them a second chance through Joshua. And this time they obeyed.

They knew what disobedience brought (see Josh. 5:6), and they learned from their ancestors' mistakes. They claimed their trust in God's plan no matter what, and He met their obedience with promise. The flow of the Jordan River stopped while they crossed, and the manna fell until they didn't need it anymore, because they had arrived in the land promised years before. But the plan wasn't over, and neither is ours.

God commanded Joshua to remove his shoes because he was standing on holy ground (see v. 15), to symbolize shedding the dirt of the lost world. And here is our blessing: *all* our pasture becomes holy ground where the Lord lives and where He is sovereign, as we learn to trust and shake off the world that would lead us astray and make us feel alone and abandoned.

The more obedient we are to God, the more we recognize and revere the holy ground on which He leads us. And when we walk in His presence, we trust Him to administer justice, to right wrongs, and to take what He's given and make it what He needs. We learn to sleep in peace in every situation, because the Shepherd has a plan.

For Reflection

How do you forgive or minister or lead as your part in God's plan?

How can you have the trust of Peter when your situation looks grim?

> *My Shepherd who grows me, please trust me with part of Your plan and make me at peace no matter what. Please help me walk on Your holy ground in obedience and trust. Amen.*

41

GROWING TRUST IN HIS CONSTANT PURSUIT OF US

And lead us not into temptation, but deliver us from the evil one.

Matthew 6:13

The story of Elisha and the axhead is another example of God's power, but it's also an example of His inexhaustible love for us.

As workers were preparing to build houses, one of them dropped an iron axhead into the Jordan. Of course it sunk, and the worker was quite upset because the axhead was borrowed. Perhaps it was also valuable. But Elisha the powerful prophet stopped to help, and all was well:

> The man of God asked, "Where did it fall?" When he showed him the place, Elisha cut a stick and threw it there, and made the iron float. "Lift it out," he said. Then the man reached out his hand and took it.
>
> 2 Kings 6:6–7

We might feel as lost as an iron axhead in a river, but if God wants to find us (and He always will), His power and promise will make it so. Still, we don't want Him to have to go so far to find us. We want to be close, easily lifted out of our darkness. Because we know temptation well, we pray for our own steps: *Please help us follow Your lead in our pasture, Lord, so we don't get lost so easily.*

And we know that cold feeling when we're still so far from the reunion with our Shepherd. We pray not to go there and then pray for His mercy when we do. Our humanness shows, but our trust grows. Instead of a smug "He'll come get me if I get lost" attitude, we have the deep desire to avoid the rescue and go straight to the renovation. We pray, *Work with me here, Lord, and keep me from falling three steps back as I take two steps forward. Save me from myself. I'm learning every day.*

> Lead me, O LORD, in your righteousness because of my enemies—
> make straight your way before me.
>
> Psalm 5:8

I'm learning I need saving from those enemies of my own making—my own doubts, fears, despair, and insecurities—so that is where I mount my defense. I can obey and grow stronger only with a connection to my Shepherd. Everything—my perspective, desires, attitude—changes when my battle station is fortified with prayer and obedience to Him.

Perhaps the Shepherd's most important directive, "Do not fear," should become mine. Knowing He's running just as hard and fast as I am when we're apart keeps me going. Knowing He will not relent, grow tired, or change His mind is all I need to know.

When we're uncertain of which course to take, we don't have to be afraid. When we're lost, we don't have to be afraid. When we're wondering if God will find us, we don't have to be afraid—because we can pray. If we've failed before, we can start again even in our despair and confusion, because *Father* is a prayer that never goes unanswered. Our Shepherd will find us and redeem us and we will learn, now and again, about His constant pursuit of us. And we don't have to be afraid.

Fear always keeps us from our pursuit of God—we fear being unworthy of His time. But He says, *No, come to Me and let Me guide you.* A disciple in no need of guidance would have no need of God. I've yet to meet one of those.

We're all in danger of getting lost again and again. We minimize the danger the more we obey our Lord, the more we rest in His presence. But we never fall off His radar, and our obedience always leads us back to Him. Our rescue starts with us lost *somewhere* and ends with us found *somewhere else*, a place He's already chosen.

For Reflection

Do you feel valuable to God, trusting Him to always fetch you out of your river of lostness?

Have you been afraid to trust Him to do that in the past?

What enemies of your own making are you fighting now, and how will you pray to your Father about them?

> *My Shepherd who grows me, please come for me always and forever. I trust in Your plan and know any fear or worry of mine isn't part of it. Please lead me to You quickly. Amen.*

42

GROWING IN OUR HEARTS
A HAVEN OF FAITH

The weapons we fight with are not the weapons of the world. On the contrary, they have divine power to demolish strongholds. We demolish arguments and every pretension that sets itself up against the knowledge of God, and we take captive every thought to make it obedient to Christ.

2 Corinthians 10:4–5

Do we learn to obey because of our faith, or does our faith grow as we obey? Perhaps the answer to both questions is yes. Somehow God meets us in the middle of our mess and leads us out. We rest in His recovery, stunned and so grateful, and we see how the plan He orchestrated works best when He's in charge.

Our faith grows deeper, and our ability and willingness to surrender to Him grows stronger. Each begets the other. And His plan for *us* advances because we're less lost, more aware of the journey, more sure of His part in it, and more sure of His direction and grace that will not end.

Growing in Waiting

Sometimes we wonder if our Shepherd's gotten a little mixed up, though, when what we expected doesn't come to pass. Those feelings of a confused sheep may be nothing new.

Joseph's brothers sold him to the Midianite merchants, who in turn sold him in Egypt to Potiphar, captain of Pharaoh's guard. Potiphar trusted Joseph and put him in charge of his whole house, but Potiphar's wife falsely accused Joseph of making advances toward her, and Potiphar threw Joseph in prison.

There Joseph's character revealed itself again, and the warden placed him in charge of other inmates. Soon the king's cupbearer and baker wound up in prison, assigned to Joseph. When Joseph interpreted the cupbearer's dream and predicted part of his future, he asked a favor in return:

> But when all goes well with you, remember me and show me kindness; mention me to Pharaoh and get me out of this prison.
>
> Genesis 40:14

Everything occurred just as Joseph had predicted. His excitement had to be tremendous as he expected to be released from the prison as he'd asked. "The chief cupbearer, however, did not remember Joseph; he forgot him" (v. 23).

The next we hear of Joseph is "two full years" later (41:1), so for 730 mornings, Joseph woke up with a decision to make: to obey or rebel, to trust or doubt, to grow or destroy, to live in his faith or get lost without it.

Through every step of his lost-and-found travels, Joseph's trust in God had grown in him a haven of faith, and his faith grew more trust as he waited through his continuing choice. Perhaps the lack of response from the cupbearer could have killed Joseph's trust like herbicide and refused to allow any more to grow. Instead Joseph, in the absence of any proof that God had abandoned him (of course, none of us will ever have any proof), grew even more ready when God called on him again, two full years later.

Joseph faced his choice—give up or grow up—and so must we. And what we learn after just the slightest inch in His direction is that God responds. It's that breath of peace you draw when you pray *Father* and know it's still enough. It works for us today because it worked for Joseph, and it worked for Peter as he slept in the jail. It also worked for Abraham: "By faith Abraham, when called to go to a place he would later receive as his inheritance, obeyed and went, even though he did not know where he was going" (Heb. 11:8).

Hearing to Grow

Joseph, Peter, Abraham—they all obeyed God because they trusted Him, and their trust grew because they obeyed Him. They surrendered their will to His because they had no doubt He knew best, that the path He had chosen would be greenest.

I try to do the same. Every day as I write my prayers to God, I include these words: "Please help me hear You in everything." I know, it sounds simple and generic, but I trust God knows exactly what to tell me and how to get through this little sheep's fuzzy understanding. I want Him to know I'm waiting for His instruction, and I don't want to miss a thing. I *know* how nearsighted I am and how easily I can overlook His work and the wonders He's placed in my path.

And I know He cares about the everyday crises of my life, so it's His input I want to hear clearly. I want Him to voice His opinion loudly in my decisions and guide me with His words when I top the next hill in the pasture. I want Him to help me put myself in His will. I want Him to be so much a part of me that I can wait for whatever He's planned, feel perfect peace in the midst of peril, and go where He leads without question. I pray, *Help me hear You. Help my trust keep me obedient and my obedience grow more trust.*

No matter what the world holds or how many wrong pastures I wander in, every moment I spend surrendering my life to my Shepherd sprouts a new dimension of my faith, and it's a glorious garden!

I grow strength and confidence, and I have answers and responses I didn't have before. The haven of faith in my heart is both created and sustained by this choice to surrender and release. Every time I surrender something of me to Him through obedience and trust—a worry, a fear, a mistake, a question, whatever—He releases me from its grip, and faith takes its place. My faith grows like kudzu on the bank, overtaking everything in its path and refusing to be contained. Our reunion begins in me something bigger than I expect.

The haven of faith in my heart is both a product and a catalyst, a miracle and a miracle maker. *Come on,* my Shepherd says, *the becoming is yet to be.* And I pray again, *Help me hear You in it all.*

For Reflection

How strong is your haven of faith? Is it as strong as Joseph's, Peter's, or Abraham's?

How do you respond to a delay—by giving up or growing up?

> *My Shepherd who grows me, please make me unafraid of any setback so that I grow more faith as I wait and work. Please help me hear You in everything. Amen.*

Part 7

Becoming

He will be the sure foundation for your times, a rich store of salvation
and wisdom and knowledge.

Isaiah 33:6

Our Shepherd grows us every day, always responding to our faith
and obedience with more growth. Our prayers keep us connected
to Him, and with our hearts open and willing and ready for more,
He takes us by the hand and shows us some of His perfect plan.
He who is everything helps us become a part of it.

Our growing never stops. We never outgrow our need for our
Shepherd's touch and direction. But we do get to enjoy some wonderful victories along the way! We see ourselves become more—
more able to understand, work, love, witness, and even guide other
lost sheep, because not so long ago we were lost too.

But we haven't become sainted sheep, and we'll get lost again,
not because we don't trust our Shepherd but because we're still

imperfect sheep. Somehow, though, our Shepherd has found a way
to work around all our fuzzy flaws, because He's decided we can
be sheep with a story to tell, a job to do, and a light to glow.

Because of His grace and willingness and complete power, I can
become an instrument for Him. Imagine—*me*, a scared and scarred
creature made secure by His love. Once lost and forever found, I
can become forever more. I can become the sheep He created me
to be and live the life He so carefully planned for me. Our reunion
makes it all possible, now and always.

Just as surely as Paul was God's "chosen instrument" with a job
to do (Acts 9:15), so are we. Our rich store from our Shepherd guar-
antees that we too have or will be given what we need to become
all He's planned. Instruments need a player. How blessed we are
that the Savior of the world came to be ours.

For Reflection

What kind of found sheep do you want to become?

What kind of story has God planned for you to tell?

> *My Shepherd who blesses me, please help me become*
> *what You already see. Release in me all You've stored*
> *so I can become a foundation for the best that's yet to*
> *be. Amen.*

43

BECOMING GOD'S INSTRUMENT OF PERSEVERANCE

As you know, we consider blessed those who have persevered.

James 5:11

Jeremiah is a complete story in perseverance. He didn't want the job God gave him, didn't find much success with it, and tried to get out of it, but he could never get lost enough to be separated from his Shepherd.

God chose Jeremiah for his job before he was even born. I believe He does the same with us, and He's just waiting for us to accept. God perseveres before we even begin.

"Before I formed you in the womb I knew you, before you were born I set you apart," God told Jeremiah (Jer. 1:5). And He tells us the same. It's hard to believe, isn't it? It was for Jeremiah too.

God needed Jeremiah to be a prophet for his nation, Israel, because the people had turned their backs on God and abandoned

Him. He persevered through Jeremiah, who was only a scared teen when the Lord gave him this great task. Like many of us when we're faced with a challenge that looks too big, he resisted and found excuses:

> "Ah, Sovereign LORD," I said, "I do not know how to speak; I am only a child." But the LORD said to me, "Do not say, 'I am only a child.' You must go to everyone I send you to and say whatever I command you. Do not be afraid of them, for I am with you and will rescue you," declares the LORD. . . . "Now, I have put my words in your mouth. See, today I appoint you over nations and kingdoms to uproot and tear down, to destroy and overthrow, to build and to plant."
>
> verses 6–10

We watch Jeremiah grow up and learn of his relationship with God through his struggles. Completely transparent, he was never afraid to complain or question because he trusted God would answer and guide him. He was aching to see that ultimate control he believed the Father had, and for forty-one years, he persevered.

Jeremiah's job wasn't easy because the Israelites didn't want to hear God's message. And Jeremiah wasn't perfect with his work. Sometimes he even tried to quit. When Pashhur the priest had Jeremiah beaten because he didn't like his prophecy of punishment for not listening to God's words, Jeremiah complained to God and wanted out.

But lost and found in the same breath, he chose to carry on, staying faithful and continuing in his calling despite the rejection and ridicule he experienced. He couldn't stop becoming the instrument the Shepherd wanted to play.

> But if I say, "I will not mention him or speak any more in his name," his word is in my heart like a fire, a fire shut up in my bones. I am weary of holding it in; indeed, I cannot.
>
> Jeremiah 20:9

We try giving up sometimes too. I've tried it lots of times with my work, when I've been disappointed or met with a cold reception. Maybe you're facing a choice like Jeremiah—to continue on in the struggle and persevere with God's charge, or to try to "not mention him" anymore. What will you do?

I wonder how the message of Jeremiah would read if he'd chosen to give up. But because he didn't, we have a perfect example of one who became an instrument of God's perseverance, so we can too. The Shepherd's promise to Jeremiah becomes our own: "'They will fight against you but will not overcome you, for I am with you and will rescue you,' declares the LORD" (Jer. 1:19).

Jeremiah complained another time, wanting to know why "the way of the wicked" prospered (Jer. 12:1). Good question, but it wasn't one God was willing to answer right then. Instead He told Jeremiah to continue his own growth:

> If you have raced with men on foot and they have worn you out, how can you compete with horses? If you stumble in safe country, how will you manage in the thickets by the Jordan?
>
> verse 5

And He tells us the same: *Handle what you've been given before you ask for more. Do well, race where you are, and persevere. Then we'll take on something bigger.*

Sure, we'd all like to fix the world, but our own backyards are the places to start. God didn't make us strong and courageous only for us to become weak and wimpy. He made us to become even more, and we get there when we don't give up.

> Let us fix our eyes on Jesus, the author and perfecter of our faith, who for the joy set before him endured the cross, scorning its shame, and sat down at the right hand of the throne of God. Consider him who endured such opposition from sinful men, so that you will not grow weary and lose heart.
>
> Hebrews 12:2–3

For Reflection

When have you, like Jeremiah, felt fearful and resistant?

What was God's response?

How did you carry on?

> *My Shepherd who blesses me, You know my fears and
> doubts when the challenge looks too big. Please help
> me persevere through all my travels to birth what
> You've already formed. Amen.*

44

BECOMING GOD'S INSTRUMENT OF FAITH

> Be my witnesses . . . to the ends of the earth.
>
> Acts 1:8

Jesus gave those who followed Him a job to do, and it wasn't easy. We read of the early Christians who were persecuted for their work, but they never gave up. They never lost faith in God and His control even when it might have seemed easy to do just that. And in at least one case, their faith found an unlikely ally in the Pharisee Gamaliel.

As more people began to believe in Jesus and follow the apostles' teachings, the Sadducees, Jewish religious leaders who denied Jesus' resurrection, were "filled with jealousy" (Acts 5:17) and threw Peter and the other apostles in jail. After the apostles were freed by an angel and were found teaching in the temple courts despite orders not to, the Sanhedrin, the Jewish elders, wanted to kill them. But they were interrupted by one of their own kind, the Pharisee Gamaliel:

> Leave these men alone! Let them go! For if their purpose or activity is of human origin, it will fail. But if it is from God, you will not be able to stop these men; you will only find yourselves fighting against God.
>
> Acts 5:38–39

Even Gamaliel, though probably not someone Peter and the others could have trusted or relied on, became an instrument of faith that moment, believing in God's complete control of our world and surrendering his actions to it. His plea was based on a trust deep enough to make him speak out in a risky way. Can we say the same?

When our own lives may seem to be screaming for drastic action like the Sanhedrin wanted, can we be like Gamaliel? Can we put our faith in God to choose what's best?

More Faith

We grow our faith as we become more attuned to the Shepherd's constant touch on our hearts, when knowledge of and belief in His control underscore our every thought. And then we want to play another part in the story—we want to become more active in living out our faith, more than Gamaliel, who spoke out in his boldness but perhaps did nothing else. We want to become like Elisha.

The faithful and obedient Elijah tutored and mentored Elisha. When Elijah knew his time on earth was almost done, he offered to grant Elisha a request. Elisha's response is one of pure faith:

> Elijah said to Elisha, "Tell me, what can I do for you before I am taken from you?"
> "Let me inherit a double portion of your spirit," Elisha replied.
>
> 2 Kings 2:9

And that's what happened. Elisha knew the job before him as the Israelites' spiritual leader would demand he become more—more capable and more connected to God than he already was. And he knew God could and would make that happen. His faith in God's plan made him take the steps he needed to take to fulfill his part. "I *know* I can do Your will, Lord, and I *know* You'll make me ready," he was saying.

God worked through His beloved Elijah and rewarded and blessed Elisha's faith. And Elisha never feared his new mission because his faith made him perfect for it.

We too are blessed and can become like Elisha. We'll receive all the tools and abilities and spirit we need for our job when we ask with Elisha's boldness and conviction and faith. We demonstrate to those around us that we're ready to become what God's planned—not because we think it's an easy thing to do but because we have faith in Him to *prepare* us. Few of us approach our Shepherd with the credentials of Elisha, but it doesn't matter. His same faith is all we need.

Our request for double portions of all we are and all we can be is a statement of our faith in God to use us in ways we can't even imagine. *I may not look like much right now,* we pray, *but God knows better and I'm trusting His plan and His control of my world, and I know I will become so much more.*

That's the prayer He's been waiting for.

For Reflection

How will you use your faith to become your Shepherd's witness where He leads?

How will you give everything to God and trust Him to do something wonderful with it?

Can you take on your mission with faith and without fear?

> *My Shepherd who blesses me, please accept the faith I have today and strengthen it for my travels to come. Please prepare me as I become more under Your control. Amen.*

45

BECOMING GOD'S
INSTRUMENT OF OBEDIENCE

> I seek you with all my heart; do not let me stray from your commands. I have hidden your word in my heart that I might not sin against you.
>
> Psalm 119:10–11

Becoming the sheep our Shepherd needs us to be means persevering through our challenges with great faith and obeying His directions. Sounds simple, doesn't it? But we know from our history how often people disobeyed the Lord, and we know from our own lives that we're not immune to disobedience either.

Maybe out of fear or confusion or something else, we follow the wrong path and get lost. But our Shepherd finds us! Then He takes that opportunity to help us learn obedience and experience its benefits. From our reunion, we discover how to become more obedient sheep, and we see how that devotion means only love and trust on our part. We discover obedience is not as complicated as we thought, and it's far more rewarding than we ever imagined.

Obeying and Being Blessed

Elijah knew the joys of that total love and devotion. He was such an instrument of obedience that he didn't even die a normal death. Elijah's obedience defined his life.

During the time Ahab was king of Israel, and in response to the people's disobedience, God sent a drought for them all, but He sent Elijah an oasis:

> "Leave here, turn eastward and hide in the Kerith Ravine, east of the Jordan. You will drink from the brook, and I have ordered the ravens to feed you there." So he did what the LORD had told him.
>
> 1 Kings 17:3–5

See that? Elijah obeyed and fled just like God told him. The ravens fed him and the brook refreshed him until God—and Elijah—didn't need it anymore (see v. 7). We'll find the same experience when we obey—our needs met through God's ready-made plan.

Do you think Elijah was scared when the brook dried up? I doubt it, because he did the very next thing his Shepherd commanded: "Go at once to Zarephath of Sidon and stay there. I have commanded a widow in that place to supply you with food" (v. 9).

This time, Elijah had a fellow sheep to grow in obedience with him—a Gentile one. The widow was about to prepare what she thought would be her and her son's last meal before they died. But her faith was stronger than her body, and she obeyed God and Elijah:

> Elijah said to her, "Don't be afraid. Go home and . . . make a small cake of bread for me . . . then make something for yourself and your son. For this is what the LORD, the God of Israel says: 'The jar of flour will not be used up and the jug of oil will not run dry until the day the LORD gives rain on the land.'" She went away and did as Elijah had told her. So

there was food every day for Elijah and for the woman and her family. For the jar of flour was not used up and the jug of oil did not run dry, in keeping with the word of the LORD spoken by Elijah.

verses 13–16

God's provision always follows our obedience; it's our own running brook when all around us is dying. His response to our love and devotion far surpasses anything we can offer, and a promise attached to our obedience is a promise we can believe in, as Caleb did.

While others who had treated the Lord with contempt were barred from the Promised Land, Caleb was brought in because of his faith and obedience. "Because my servant Caleb has a different spirit and follows me wholeheartedly, I will bring him into the land he went to, and his descendants will inherit it" (Num. 14:24).

To follow our Shepherd wholeheartedly is to obey Him, and it's never too late to start, to become a sheep like Caleb. And Paul gives us even more to go on. He says the kingdom of God is a matter of "righteousness, peace and joy in the Holy Spirit" (Rom. 14:17). I know that list doesn't include obedience by name, but that's what underlies all the rest.

God creates us new and righteous when He finds and rescues us, and He makes us whole and free. The lostness is gone, but the pasture full of choices remains. Our reunion and redemption create in us hearts acutely aware of their choice to follow and bound only by their devotion—hearts that obey not because they have to but because they want to.

God creates a peace for us we can also choose—or not. That peace—internally between us and God and externally as we deal with others and live our tangible lives—is a direct result of our obedience. We cannot feel peace if any part of us is stumbling astray. We cannot be in two places at once. We know God's peace simply when we're following Him.

Finally, we may wonder why Paul saw joy as so important. Perhaps it's because true joy can come from only one place—our

Shepherd's arms. Sure, we can be *happy* about things that come and go, but *pure joy* is the choice to believe and celebrate when we can as well as when we can't see the work and wonder of God. Our obedience to surrender and to trust in His control no matter what creates in us a joy that lets us become sheep who can walk both in the valleys and over the hills, devoted to a Shepherd of love and grace.

And there's a bonus—the other sheep see us as we obey and serve in joy and peace because God's righteousness made us new and allows us to become more. We can make it simple for them too.

Shout for joy to the LORD, all the earth. Worship the LORD with gladness; come before him with joyful songs.

Psalm 100:1–2

For Reflection

How do you obey God, and how are you likely to disobey?

How has God blessed you in response to your obedience?

How can you follow Paul's thoughts on righteousness, peace, and joy?

My Shepherd who blesses me, please help me obey when I am weak. Show me how to follow You in all things and experience the peace only You can provide. Amen.

46

BECOMING GOD'S
INSTRUMENT OF SERVICE

Command them to do good, to be rich in good deeds, and to be generous and willing to share. In this way they will lay up treasure for themselves as a firm foundation for the coming age, so that they may take hold of the life that is truly life.

1 Timothy 6:18–19

Our perseverance commits us to serve, our faith makes us willing, and our obedience makes us able. Like everything else, our service to our Shepherd is our choice. And it's the way to "life that is truly life," because service is another word for worship.

The whole story of Nehemiah is a story of worship. It is tangible service wrapped in dogged perseverance, tested faith, and unfaltering obedience. Remember, he and the Israelites rebuilt the walls of Jerusalem despite the worst odds. It's a dramatic example of sheep being found and redeemed, and through their *service* becoming everything their Shepherd believed they could. He waits for a similar celebration with us.

And He has other blessings stored up we don't even know about yet. Just keep worshiping, He says. "Never be lacking in zeal, but keep your spiritual fervor, serving the Lord. Be joyful in hope, patient in affliction, faithful in prayer" (Rom. 12:11–12).

Maybe He sends the reminder because He thinks we'll get sidetracked between big projects and opportunities to serve and lose our devotion and enthusiasm. Maybe He's right. We can sometimes overlook the small "service projects" or fail to equate every action with worship. What a loss.

Because we can't truly serve God without worshiping Him, and because our service—in gratitude for His care and guidance and in awe of His grace and grandeur—is a step in His tracks, we serve by giving. We give what we are and everything we'll become.

We're in a pasture full of needs only we can meet. Nothing is insignificant, and everything builds on everything else to produce great blessings all around. To us, our service is big sometimes and small sometimes, but to our Shepherd, it is all worship, complete belief, and acceptance of His control.

If we thought otherwise, we couldn't do a thing. And as we grow and become, we will do so many more things! Sometimes we'll see the bigger picture—the raising of children or the reaching of unbelievers. That's serving God and we know it.

Other times, we'll never see how the silent prayer for the stranger we met today turned out or know if our overheard testimony touched someone, but that's okay. We can trust that blink of service was also part of God's great plan. We can be confident that anything we give out of worship as we follow our Shepherd will be an instrument of service exactly where He needs it.

The *why* of our service comes from us. The *how* comes from God. Only through the "incomparable riches of his grace" (Eph. 2:7) can we build a wall or raise a child or forgive a hurt or encourage a friend. Only through His grace in our travels do we become the servant sheep He desires. His command of the world extends to us and equips us to answer every call of our name.

Lord, you establish peace for us; all that we have accomplished you have done for us.

Isaiah 26:12

For Reflection

How do you worship through your service to your Shepherd?

Do you get sidetracked between big projects?

What small projects might you have overlooked?

*My Shepherd who blesses me, please never let me
forget or neglect the opportunities to serve You.
Please help me see every day a new way to become the
servant sheep who trusts in Your great plan. Amen.*

47

BECOMING GOD'S
INSTRUMENT OF GRACE

From the fullness of his grace we have all received one blessing
after another.

John 1:16

David understood well the power and generosity of God's grace.
And he knew he could do and be nothing without it. Close to his
death, as the Israelites prepared to build the temple in Jerusalem,
David through his prayer reminded the people of their place in
God's world, His sovereignty, and their blessing to become a part
of His plans.

Yours, O LORD, is the greatness and the power and the glory and
the majesty and the splendor, for everything in heaven and earth is
yours. . . . Everything comes from you, and we have given you only
what comes from your hand.

1 Chronicles 29:11, 14

We understand that truth too as we travel from lost to found, see how much we've grown, and cherish what waits for us to become. And we see even more of our Shepherd's delight to be close to us, because He is the giver of all things, including everything we create or ways we serve or gifts we use. It's all His to begin and end with, and His grace allows us to be the vessels, because He wants that relationship with us that only grace allows.

We'll never be as good as God or as smart as God or capable of anything outside of God, but His grace grows us to become as much like Him as possible. Understanding that crucial dependency keeps us following where He leads. We want to know what'll happen next, and God sets no limits, even working with the scattered and sometimes unreliable sheep that we are.

Beginning Now and Again

Paul understood God's grace and became a powerful example of His particular affection for and abilities with the lost and found. Paul recognized his chance, through no skill of his own, to be an instrument of God's grace in all his work. Everything began and became because God first made it so:

> I became a servant of this gospel by the gift of God's grace given me through the working of his power.
>
> Ephesians 3:7

No matter who we are or how lost we've been, the grace to find us and then grow us is already there. God's grace is boundless, and He waits for us to become a part of something wonderful He's already planned. We do that by giving back what's His.

The business you want to start is God's business too. The degree you want to earn is God's degree too. The skill you want to learn is God's skill too. You will grow and become through those experiences and many more because God's grace guides you through your travels, and His sense of direction never fails. Everything built on His grace keeps building.

When we live as an instrument of His grace, we live out what we've been given. Do you think He's shorted you, will fail to prepare you, will hold back a little something for fun? No! God's grace is sufficient to let us become everything He already sees. We're just giving it back in everything we do.

When we see and claim that relationship of oneness with our Shepherd, we claim His promise to supply all the grace we need for everything we see before us. And a thousand other promises follow. Our becoming becomes another one.

> Behold, I will create new heavens and a new earth. The former things will not be remembered, nor will they come to mind. But be glad and rejoice forever in what I will create.
>
> Isaiah 65:17–18

For Reflection

How do you live out God's grace in what you do?

Why do you ever feel lacking in all you need, and how do you talk to God about that?

My Shepherd who blesses me, I'm so thankful for
Your grace! Please help me understand its power and
use all You've given me to become more than I could
ever see on my own. Amen.

48

BECOMING GOD'S INSTRUMENT OF PROMISE

Be strong and very courageous. Be careful to obey all the law my servant Moses gave you; do not turn from it to the right or to the left, that you may be successful wherever you go. . . . Do not be terrified; do not be discouraged, for the LORD your God will be with you wherever you go.

Joshua 1:7, 9

With the promise of God's grace, how can we fail to become all He's planned? We have no excuse! His grace makes all things possible, so He can find us and rescue us and grow us into the exact sheep He needs in His pasture. Sounds like He does all the work, doesn't it?

No, we have a very critical role—we must *believe* His promises to make them real to us. We must choose to follow our Shepherd and believe His promises of a new life, a new direction, and a new purpose. That's how He works. "See, I am doing a new thing! Now it springs up; do you not perceive it?" (Isa. 43:19).

We all have those times of doubt when what God promised and what we see or feel look different. That's just our limited sheep thinking, looking only at what's in front of us, forgetting the underlying grace we know sustains all. Holding onto our Shepherd's promises when a child has turned away, a dream has died, or a friend has betrayed us—that's the part of our becoming when we *believe still*.

That's when everything we do and are is anchored and supported in God's promises no matter what. No matter how lost we feel, we can look at all the hell before us and yet remind ourselves with true conviction, *"He promised!* He promised to find me and love me and guide me forever and ever." And with that, we become more.

The promise God made to Abraham of having descendants came to be because it was a promise, not a rule or statute. Paul explained, "For if the inheritance depends on the law, then it no longer depends on a promise; but God in his grace gave it to Abraham through a promise" (Gal. 3:18). And we know how Abraham responded:

> He did not waver through unbelief regarding the promise of God, but was strengthened in his faith and gave glory to God, being fully persuaded that God had power to do what he had promised.
>
> Romans 4:20–21

That choice to *believe* becomes one we live with every breath. His promises of love and grace let me become what you see: a sheep found, and a promise for you too.

Whatever He promises, His grace has already made possible, and our purpose lives on. We are found, and it's only the beginning.

For Reflection

How do you feel when you truly believe God will always be faithful to His promises?

What promises are you claiming today, and how will you let others see them in your life?

> *My Shepherd who blesses me, thank You for Your*
> *promises, for Your character that doesn't change.*
> *Please help me believe You and follow You to become*
> *part of Your promise. Amen.*

49

BECOMING GOD'S
INSTRUMENT OF PURPOSE

The plans of the LORD stand firm forever, the purposes of his heart through all generations.

Psalm 33:11

Purpose is such a loaded word. It can seem heavy with obligation, as if some massive undertaking is waiting for us and there'll be no peace until this dreaded thing is done and put away, stamped finished so we can take a break. Yet we miss so much when we look at purpose that way.

Our purpose is not to somehow *live through* some tough assignment but to joyfully *live in* the pasture of our Shepherd. It's not a list of chores to be crossed off but a walk of faith to be run with our Rescuer. There's no beginning and no end, just restarts at our reunions, when we become more the disciple our Lord sees all along.

Does that mean uprooting ourselves and moving across the country? Maybe, but most likely it means uprooting our minds from their place of tiresome acceptance and moving our lives more in line with God's fascinating design for them.

Seeing First

I can't see with the infinite and unmistakable vision and power of our Shepherd, but I can see before I can touch sometimes. I know you can too. Any purpose you've ever fulfilled, God had to make clear in your heart first. And that first revealing picture you saw grew and became the very thing you knew it could, though nobody else could see it.

When I begin a new book and look with my heart, I see it already finished, ready for a reader, before I ever write a word. You also see your way in whatever calls you, and it all works to fulfill His purposes through you. I wonder if God allows us to understand that order so we'll see what He's capable of doing with us—how He sees beyond today to what we'll become tomorrow.

We play our parts when we allow His pictures to come to life in us, when we keep following Him in the steps He's made just for us. Our becoming keeps growing.

> Now finish the work, so that your eager willingness to do it may be matched by your completion of it, according to your means. For if the willingness is there, the gift is acceptable.
>
> 2 Corinthians 8:11–12

Sometimes I'm a Quilt

One day I decided I'd make a quilt. Now, I'd never made a quilt before, but that seemed like an insignificant detail because I could see in my heart what I wanted the finished product to be before I ever threaded a needle. And I didn't get an easy, predictable pattern to follow (if there is such a thing) because that wasn't my picture.

No, I decided I wanted to quilt the picture from the front of a greeting card. It didn't seem like it would be that complicated—a little bear in a dress carrying a pot of flowers . . . how hard could it be? Cut a few pieces of fabric, sew them together, and voilà—a quilt!

I hear you laughing. I did everything you can do to a quilt wrong. Many times I had to walk away so my mind might uncover an answer. I ran out of fabric a couple times, and I couldn't get more pieces of some of it. I was beginning to wonder if what I saw in my heart would ever be real. But I never considered giving up.

Finally, the thousand pieces of fabric and million yards of thread became a quilt. Finally, it surrendered to me and I was in control. Finally, the quilt became real, and a part of me lives in it still.

I can be as stubborn with God as my quilt was with me sometimes (okay, often), but God never gives up. I keep telling Him that He could have made me easier to deal with, but He says that'd be too predictable. He knows great purposes for me and won't let me abandon them, no matter how many times He has to stitch me over to get me right.

Every reunion brings a new and wonderful purpose, a new picture to follow, a new joy to live. Maybe you're a quilt sometimes too. That's okay. The Shepherd's hands and heart are made for turning scattered and uneven bits into something beautiful. He makes all the pieces fit when we surrender to His control.

> The LORD will fulfill his purpose for me; your love, O LORD, endures forever—do not abandon the works of your hands. . . . You hem me in—behind and before; you have laid your hand upon me.
>
> Psalm 138:8; 139:5

God's already planned every purpose for your life like a perfectly packed suitcase, so every wonderful thing you are is there for you to bring to light. The only ingredient you supply is your faith in His power to make your purposes real—then He works with what He has: you, a single little sheep, to do the work of the Shepherd.

With our *perseverance, faith, obedience,* and *service* through God's *grace,* His *promise* is lived out in our *purpose.* Through a lowly sheep, the designs of the Shepherd come to life in a world apt to get lost. And once lost herself, the found sheep grows and becomes everything her Shepherd knew she could.

Wholly loved and never abandoned, she follows unafraid, for she trusts in her Shepherd to lead her safely, and her travels become her testimony.

"Follow Me," He says. And she can imagine no other way.

He will stand and shepherd his flock in the strength of the Lord, in the majesty of the name of the Lord his God. And they will live securely, for then his greatness will reach to the ends of the earth. And he will be their peace.

Micah 5:4–5

For Reflection

What do you think about when you consider God's purposes for your future? What purposes have you fulfilled in the past?

What purpose comes to mind most easily, and what do you see? What is your first step in living it?

> *My Shepherd who blesses me, please help me live every amazing purpose You've already planned for me. Lead me boldly on this lost-and-found journey, always closer to You. Amen.*

Karon Phillips Goodman is a speaker and the author of several books, including *Another Fine Mess, Lord! You Still Here, Lord?* and *You're Late Again, Lord!* She lives in Alabama.